Representing America

Representing America

The Citizen and the Professional Legislator in the House of Representatives

Rebekah Herrick and Samuel H. Fisher III

LEXINGTON BOOKS

A division of
ROWMAN & LITTLEFIELD PUBLISHERS, INC.
Lanham • Boulder • New York • Toronto • Plymouth, UK

LEXINGTON BOOKS

A division of Rowman & Littlefield Publishers, Inc.
A wholly owned subsidiary of The Rowman & Littlefield Publishing Group, Inc.
4501 Forbes Boulevard, Suite 200
Lanham, MD 20706

Estover Road
Plymouth PL6 7PY
United Kingdom

British Library Cataloguing in Publication Information Available

Library of Congress Cataloging-in-Publication Data

Herrick, Rebekah, 1960–
  Representing America : the citizen and the professional legislator in the House of
Representatives / Rebekah Herrick and Samuel H. Fisher.
    p. cm.
  Includes bibliographical references and index.
  ISBN-13: 978-0-7391-1727-9 (cloth : alk. paper)
  ISBN-10: 0-7391-1727-0 (cloth : alk. paper)
  1. United States. Congress. House. 2. United States. Congress. House—Constituent
communication. 3. Legislators—United States. 4. Representative government and
representation—United States. 5. Political participation—United States. I. Fisher,
Samuel H., 1955– II. Title.
  JK1319.H47 2007
  328.73'072—dc22   2007005721

Printed in the United States of America

♾™ The paper used in this publication meets the minimum requirements of American
National Standard for Information Sciences—Permanence of Paper for Printed Library
Materials, ANSI/NISO Z39.48–1992.

With great delight we dedicate this book to our children, Neal and Reece Franklin, and Ben and Jacob Fisher

Table of Contents

List of Tables

Introduction

The catalyst for this book was the term limits movement of the 1990s and the ensuing debate both in the public and among scholars. Term limit advocates viewed term limits as the key to replacing professional legislators with citizen legislators. Citizen legislators were preferred because they would improve congressional responsiveness to the people.[1] Since they are first and foremost private citizens, they have work and life experiences similar to most Americans, and theoretically they have a better idea of citizens' interests than Washington professionals. During House debate on term limits, Rep. Ronald Packard (R-IN) stated, "But the real experience that is important in this job is the experience we bring to the job, the experience of having been teachers, farmers, or businessmen" (*Congressional Record* 1995, H3924). Because they will one day return to the status of private citizen, they will have to live under the rules they create and thus will be more sensitive to the impact laws have on most Americans. George Will, a noted political commentator, states, "Many Americans wish that a lot of legislators had a better sense of American life, and particularly of what it is like to be on the receiving end of the high-minded laws and regulations that gush like a cataract from Washington" (Will 1993, 200-201). Another line of reasoning stems from the assumption that citizen legislators have unique goals and desires for serving in political office. While citizen legislators are thought to serve out of a motivation to achieve good public policy, professional politicians are thought to be motivated by advancing their political careers (political ambition), not good public policy. Professional legislators are also thought to be more susceptible to corruption. The longer one stays in politics, the greater the temptation and opportunity to substitute one's personal goals for the public's good.

However, the desire for a return to citizen legislators with limited political careers was not universal. Term limits critics believed that professional legislators were more responsive and better able to represent constituents—opposite the argument for term limits. It is long service that gives professional legislators greater legislative knowledge and experience, making them better able to craft effective policy. Only individuals interested in reelection are held accountable by elections. Term limits would result in members unconcerned about pleasing their voters and more concerned about pushing their own political agenda during their short stay. According to Rep. James Sensenbrenner (R-WI):

> In fact term limits will actually make Representatives and Senators more distant from their constituents, because they will no longer have the incentive to go back home and face their people and find out what their people are thinking

in order to win reelection. . . . Finally, term limits and changing the Constitution will not change human nature. Human beings are those who are elected by the people to represent them in the Congress of the United States. The reward for doing a good job in this business is reelection, and that is an incentive that drives us to represent our people and go back home and listen to what the people are saying (*Congressional Record* 1995, H3893).

Although the term limits movement is on life support, an examination of the differences between citizen and professional legislators is still a very worthwhile endeavor. First, even if the term limits movement is weaker than fifteen years ago, the debates continue. Several states have considered removing term limits, and in Utah and Idaho the legislature has removed them. Second, the desire for politicians having short limits has dominated U.S. history. Petracca (1992) describes how the federalists and anti-federalists debated term limits and that prior to the Civil War there was often a voluntary rotation of office and several states enacted laws requiring rotation of office, usually for executive posts. It was not until the twentieth century that long service in legislative and other posts became common. Third, the call for term limits or return to citizen legislators is likely to resurface. Perceptions of an unresponsive, fiscally irresponsible, and politically corrupt Congress helped spur the term limits movement in the 1990s. Charges of corruption and fiscal irresponsibility in Congress are reemerging, and if history repeats itself, this will lead to renewed calls for term limits.

Also there are important theoretical issues that transcend the debates over term limits. The crux of the debate concerns how experience and ambition affect legislator's ability to represent constituents. Does political experience give politicians greater understanding and insight into the needs of their constituents, or does it give them feeling of privilege and entitlement that distances them from their constituents? Does the desire for a political career (ambition) encourage politicians to serve their constituents in order to get reelected? Does the desire for reelection encourage politicians to serve the voters or does it make them serve special interests who donate to their campaigns? Or rather yet, are politicians so secure in their reelection prospects that elections serve little function except in open seat races?

In addition to the importance of understanding whether citizen or professional legislators are better representatives, there is a unique opportunity to explore these issues in the modern Congress because of the term limits movement of the 1990s. During the 1990s, in response to the desire for citizen legislators, two phenomena occurred that increased the number of legislators that could be considered citizen legislators. As we discuss in the first chapter we define citizen legislators as those who do not see politics as their primary career. We subdivide citizen legislators into two types: those who have little previous political experience—retrospective citizen legislators—and those who do not plan a long future in politics—prospective citizen legislators. First, there was a rise in the number of legislators who came to office with little or no political experience, or could be seen as retrospective citizen legislators. In the 101st Congress (1991), ninety-four House members listed public service as their occupation; this fell to sixty-seven in the following congress (Ornstein, Mann, and Malbin 2002, 43). Second, fifty members entering Congress in the 1990s signed a pledge to limit their terms in the House. This gives a pool of members who could be classified as prospective citizen legislators.

While the authors acknowledge their responsibility for any mistakes, we must acknowledge the support provided to us during the process. Oklahoma State University granted Rebekah a sabbatical, and she spent the time as a visiting scholar at the University of South Alabama. The University of South Alabama granted Sam a sabbatical, which he spent conducting interviews in Washington, D.C., and working in Tulsa, Oklahoma, where we finished the first draft of the manuscript. Dr. John Smykla, former chair of the Department of Political Science and Criminal Justice at the University of South Alabama, provided generous travel support and encouragement for the project. Marilyn Fisher, Sam's spouse, and Lori Franklin, Rebekah's partner, reread and edited many versions of the manuscript. They took on this task with great humor and patience. We also wish to thank those who offered us input at various stages of the project: John Hibbing, Jim Woods, Emily Herrick, and Ray Tatalovich. Also, thanks to Christina Busse for copy editing the manuscript. Finally, a special thanks to those who allowed us to interview them and to Artemesia Stanberry and Rep. Jo Bonner (District 1 Alabama) for helping us set up interviews.

Notes

1. This is somewhat of an oversimplification since some term limit advocates, such as George Will, thought term limits were preferred because they would make members less responsive to citizens' short term desires.

Chapter One
Are Citizen Legislators More Responsive Than Professional Legislators?

Throughout the past hundred years there has been a dramatic rise in the number of professional politicians in Congress. Until 1901, 42.9 percent of House members served just a single term, 53 percent served between two and six terms, and House members served a mean of 2.2 terms (Huckabee 2002). Between the 80th Congress (1947) and 107th Congress (2002) the mean number of terms served more than doubled to 5.8 terms. Similarly, while in the 1950s no member listed politics or public service as an occupation, in the 107th Congress 126 members listed public service as their occupation (Ornstein, Mann, and Malbin 2002, 43). By the 1990s, Americans had a negative view of the growth of professional politicians. They were viewed as out of touch with their constituents, immune to political shifts in the electorate, indebted to special interests, and corrupt. Support for Congress plummeted. There was a call to return Congress to what many saw as the original model—a body composed of private citizens who serve and then quickly return to their home states and their private careers. Rep. Ernest Istook (R-OK) offered up the example of citizen legislators during debate on term limits in the House, "This country was founded by those who set aside, for so long as was necessary, their individual businesses and pursuits, but never intending to become a professional political class. They brought with them the variety of strengths, backgrounds, and insights which can only be gained from interaction with fellow citizens on a normal, everyday basis" (*Congressional Record* 1995, H3917). A movement to limit the number of terms that members of Congress could serve was invigorated. More than a dozen states passed legislation to limit the terms of their states' elected federal officials although the Supreme Court in *U.S. Term Limits, Inc. v. Thornton* (1995) ruled such laws unconstitutional.

What is unclear is to what degree, if any, citizen and professional legislators differ in their approach to legislating and representing their constituents. Are citizen legislators better able to understand the people's needs and the effects of laws on them because they have experiences as private citizens? Are they better able to work on serving the real needs of citizens because they are less interested in pursuing their own political careers? Or are they less able to work on legislation that is beneficial to the people because they do not have experience representing others? Are they less accountable to the people because they are less interested in a future in politics and thus less concerned about reelection?

This book examines the similarities of and differences between professional legislators and citizen legislators with a focus on representation. We define professional legislators as legislators who see their primary vocation as politics, and citizen legislators as those who do not. Citizen legislators have greater interest in politics than average Americans, who are generally disinterested and inactive in politics, but are less focused on politics as a career than are professional politicians who see politics as their primary occupation, if not their way of life. Within this definition of citizen legislators the key factor separating them from professional legislators is how long they want to work in politics. When conceptualizing a legislator's desired time in politics there are two approaches: prospective (the desire for a future career in politics) and retrospective (a history of political experience).[1] Prospective professional legislators come into office planning to spend the foreseeable future in a political career while prospective citizen legislators come into office intending to serve a limited number of terms. Retrospective professional legislators come into office with extensive prior political experience having had a career in politics while retrospective citizen legislators come into office with little or no prior political experience. As we will discuss later, the ambition for a future in politics has often been argued to affect legislative behavior (see Schlesinger 1966, for a discussion of ambition theory). Some political observers see this drive for future office as forcing legislators to make poor policy decisions for short term political gain or serving special interests for electoral help (for example, see Mayhew 1974 and Armor 1994) while others see the drive as forcing legislators to be accountable to the people (for example, see Schlesinger 1966; Hamilton, Madison, and Jay 1976). Also, as we will discuss later, whether previous political experience is a liability or an asset is a contentious debate. According to Rep. Ronald Packard (R-IN), "Some people cite the loss of experience as the most important reason to defeat term limits. But the real experience that is important in this job is the experience we bring to the job, the experience of having been teachers, farmers, or businessmen" (*Congressional Record* 1995, H3924). On the other hand, some believe experience is necessary to help legislators develop the skills and knowledge needed to effectively legislate in the interests of the people (for example, see Berkman 1993).

The stability of political career goals is unclear. It is likely some members have stable political ambitions. They have always wanted a political career and always will. However, some enter Congress planning to stay for an indefinite amount of time but find the job undesirable. Some may enter planning to stay a short time but love the job and end up staying longer. Accordingly, our definition assumes that over the course of a lifetime people may change their political ambitions. Some politicians may share the qualities of both retrospective and prospective professional legislators, and some may share the qualities of both retrospective and prospective citizen legislators. But we do assume at least some stability. Members are unlikely to change their minds about their future immediately upon arrival. If career ambitions were too fluid they would be unlikely to have explanatory value.

This book uses both definitions of citizen legislators, prospective and retrospective, to test whether citizen legislators differ from others in their representational styles. We do this by examining the members elected to the House of Representatives in the 1990s. This is a decade that saw a rise in prospective and retrospective citizen legislators. Having defined citizen legislators and professional legislators, our next task is to explain what is meant by representation.

What is Representation?

At its core, representation involves making present something that is otherwise not present (Pitkin 1967). Within this very broad definition, Pitkin identifies four ways to conceptualize representation; two of these, descriptive and substantive, are most relevant here.[2] Descriptive representation requires a representative assembly to be a replica of the thing being made present, such as a portrait, mirror, or map (Pitkin 1967, 60-91). Consequently, for Congress to have a high level of descriptive representation, the demographic make-up of Congress must have proportions similar to the key demographic characteristics of the American people. Although it is assumed that legislatures with high levels of descriptive representation will act in the interests of the people, there is no such explicit requirement with descriptive representation. Even though the legislative body "looks" like the population, it does not necessarily follow that the legislature will reflect the interests of the population.

The second type of representation, substantive or acting for representation, requires members to act in the interests of the represented (Pitkin 1967, 114). With descriptive representation, that which is being made present is being made present in character, while with substantive or acting for representation, that which is being made present is being made present in action. Representing here means acting in the interest of the represented, in a manner responsive to them. The representative must act independently using his own discretion and judgment and he must be the one who acts. The represented must also be conceived as capable of independent action and judgment, not merely being taken care of. And despite the resulting potential for conflict between representative and represented about what is to be done, that conflict must not normally take place (Pitkin 1967, 207).

A key contemporary debate surrounding representation is the relative importance of descriptive representation. Most acknowledge that descriptive representation is valuable if it increases substantive representation. Do women better represent women, blacks better represent blacks, and so on? There are two reasons why it may increase substantive representation. First, descriptive representation enhances the likelihood that all voices are heard in political debates. Pitkin (1967) states that descriptive representation allows different types of people to bring in their unique experiences and knowledge. Legislators who possess different characteristics likely have different experiences and possess different information to bring into discussions on legislation and policy. For example, congresswomen bring insights to legislative debates on women's issues that are often missed by congressmen (Kathlene 1995; Aved, Levy, and Tein 2001; Walsh 2002). Providing insights or information that only individuals with certain characteristics are likely to have improves debate and legislative action by increasing the chances that all views and relevant information are included. Likewise, another way increased descriptive representation can lead to improved substantive representation is through surrogate representation. Mansbridge (1999, 2003) writes of surrogate representation as representation without an electoral relationship. It occurs when members represent a group of people who do not necessarily reside in their districts. An example is black legislators representing black interests that are not tied to their particular districts. She notes that surrogate representation can become strong when a representative shares the experiences with a constituency that is underrepresented (2003, 523). These legislators may have pressure put on them to be active by people sharing their minority status. They also identify with the needs of the people sharing their minority status making them acutely aware of policy needs. Thus representatives who are poor, of a racial, religious, or ethnic minority, or female may feel a need to represent these groups.

Whether descriptive representation of "out-groups" leads to their substantive representation is contested. The literature on the effects of gender and race/ethnicity on legislative behavior helps to illustrate the point. This literature indicates that women in Congress and in state legislatures are more likely to support and prioritize issues of specific interest to women than are male legislators (Bingham 1997; Dolan 1997; Foerstel and Foerstel 1996; Gertzog 1995; Swers 2001, 2002; Thomas 1994; Vega and Firestone 1995; Wolbrecht 2002). As the number of women in a legislature increases, its legislative agenda becomes more likely to reflect the interests of women (Foerstel and Foerstel 1996; Gertzog 1995; Thomas 1994). These studies lend support to the view that descriptive representation has positive effects on the discussion of legislative issues. However, while these differences tend to be statistically significant, they are often fairly small substantively, paling in comparison to the policy differences between members of the different parties (see Reingold 2000 for a critical view of the idea that gender matters). A key reason women may be limited in their ability to focus on women's issues is that they need to represent the interests of their male constituents as well as their female constituents to win reelection. Also, women differ among themselves on issues. Not every woman is of the same opinion on traditional women's issues such as family leave, abortion, healthcare, and workplace discrimination. The research on whether blacks are better represented by black House members and the literature on whether Latinos are better represented by Latinos also has been mixed. Swain (1993) and Hero and Tolbert (1995) find that members' race/ethnicity has little independent effect on voting for issues of interest to blacks and Latinos. However, Tate (2003), Canon (1999), and Kerr and Miller (1997) find that members' race/ethnicity has important independent effects on the representation of black and Latino interests. Whether a shared social characteristic, such as gender or ethnicity, between the representative and the represented indicates a shared agreement on issues may be thought of as contextual or a matter of degree. Having a representative share your characteristics may increase your voice, but it may not be the most significant factor.

Descriptive representation may be important, even if it has small direct effects on substantive representation, if it affects the relationship constituents have with their members in a positive manner. There is evidence that such an effect exists. If constituents share the race of their representative they are more likely to contact their representative (Gay 2002), and have more positive perceptions of their members (Gay 2002; Tate 2001, 2003). However, sharing the race of their representative is not empowering; that is, it does necessarily generate more interest in politics (Tate 2003). If constituents share the gender of their representative they too have more positive evaluations of their member but are not more engaged or supportive of the government generally (Lawless 2004). Descriptive representation can also increase the political efficacy of the represented (Emig, Hesse, and Fisher 1996) and the number and diversity of people seeking office. Members who have characteristics of "out-groups" serve as role models. As more women and minorities enter politics, more women and minorities are likely to see holding elective office as an option, increasing the pool of individuals who may seek political office. Thus, if citizen legislators are more likely to be similar to the people and descriptive representation improves representation, then citizen legislators will offer better representation.

Although the importance of substantive representation is less debatable, there are questions about what constitutes substantive representation. Often it is thought of as making policy decisions, but there are other ways members can act for the represented. Members can be involved in pork-barreling and constituent services. Members can help individual constituents solve problems and in that way act on their behalf, and they can procure money for district projects that may provide a service or increase employment in the district. The key with substantive representation is that representatives are to act in their constituents' interests. A question that follows from this is, "how do representatives know what that interest is?" The question normally is presented with two possible variants—delegate (mandate) and trustee (independence). Legislators can be seen as strictly delegates who translate their constituents' wishes into policies or they can act as trustees who decide in their own minds what is best for their constituents. As Pitkin's quote above suggests, there generally should not be a conflict between the two (assuming people know their interests), but philosophers debate which is ideal.[3] In particular when the two diverge, the representative must be able to defend going against the wishes of the constituency.

Closely tied to the discernment of constituent preferences is deciding the place of those desires within the larger and conflicting interests of the nation. Should a representative narrowly focus on the district's interests, or should the representative's focus expand to include the general interests of the nation? Generally in the United States, the legislative structure supports the notion that legislators focus on their district's needs. Members are elected and voted out of office by a district, not by the nation. This makes them accountable to their district.

One way for representatives to know and make decisions in the interests of the represented is for members to keep in contact with their constituents. Since Fenno (1977) discussed members' home styles, congressional scholars have recognized that representation involves staying in contact with constituents. Fenno, as well as others (see for example, Hibbing 1991), examined the frequency of members' trips to the district, and their allocation of staff in the district as a means of estimating which members more actively keep in touch with their constituents. The basic idea is that members who spend time back home and have more staff in the district will better understand the concerns and interests of the district. Additionally, constituent contact offers members an opportunity to explain their Washington activities to their constituents (Fenno 1977). Representation is more than reflecting the view of constituents but it also "help[s] bring constituents into the process and to unite them into a coherent political whole" (Tate 2003, 132-33).

Also affecting representation is whether members are active and effective legislators. Even members who completely understand the interests of their constituents and want to advance those interests are not going to be effective legislators if they do not know how to legislate. Members who put minimal work into legislation are not doing what needs to be done in order to make present their constituents' interests. The better able members are to shape the outcome of legislative debates/votes, the better able they are to represent their constituents. Simply, members who draft legislation designed to aid their constituents without being able to see that legislation passed, have not helped their constituents anymore than the ones who do nothing or help some other interest.

Acting on behalf of constituents also requires that members behave ethically. By being ethical we mean that members behave in ways that support the legislative process. For example, a key principle of ethical legislative behavior is what Thompson (1995) calls independence:[4] basing decisions primarily on the merits of the policy under consideration.[5] According to this principle, when evaluating policies, legislators may consider a variety of factors, such as the opinions of their constituents and the stated positions of their political party. However members should not be influenced by opinions and forces irrelevant to deliberations, such as advancing members' career goals or helping campaign donors, except as they may relate to representing constituents' interests.

Are Citizen or Professional Legislators Better Representatives?

Arguments made as to why citizen legislators should be better or worse at representing the interests of their constituents tend to focus on two issues. The first has greater relevance for prospective citizen legislators and concerns the value of political ambition and, relatedly, elections. The second has greater relevance for retrospective citizen legislators and concerns whether private sector or political experience is preferred. Generally, we believe that political experience is of considerable value and that political ambition and elections help keep members' accountable. However, we also believe that other factors help to minimize the differences between citizen and professional legislators, whether prospective or retrospective.

One potential value of citizen legislators who come from the private sector, that is, retrospective citizen legislators, is that they better understand their constituents' preferences. Since retrospective citizen legislators have "walked in the same shoes" as constituents, it is argued, they have a better understanding of how laws affect Americans' daily lives. In part, they are more likely to be similar to the people or offer better descriptive representation. Thus, if descriptive representation improved substantive representation then citizen legislators would be better.[6]

Prospective citizen legislators too may be closer to the people because they plan to return to private life, and, as a consequence, they are more likely to be concerned with how laws will affect Americans' daily lives. Since prospective citizen legislators return to the private sector to be subject to government laws and regulations, they will exercise greater scrutiny of the proposed acts of government. In contrast, a professional politician concerned about reelection and maintaining power will not be sensitive to the legislation's impact and thus be less inclined to make the right choice for the district.

One problem with expecting citizen legislators to better mirror America is that it assumes that a large number of ordinary Americans want to serve and that voters want to be represented by their neighbors, co-workers, and even employees. However, these assumptions seem unlikely in an electoral system that requires much of candidates and a job that requires either uprooting families or maintaining two households, and subjecting the member and family to considerable media scrutiny. Fowler (1992, 182-83) argues that term limits, which yield prospective citizen legislators, are unlikely to change the type of person elected to office, since Americans have elected wealthy white males, whose profession is likely the law, to Congress for two hundred years. She notes that even when norms required voluntary limits, Congress was composed of these types of individuals. Additionally, she argues that because of the resources needed to successfully campaign for office, it is unlikely that other types of people, primarily less affluent or less well connected, will be elected. Carroll and Jenkins's (2001) research on the effects of term limits on the election of women illustrates the problems. They examined the election of women to state legislatures after the enactment of term limits and found that after an initial jump in the number of women elected, that number declined. The reason they declined was because there were not enough women seeking new seats to replace the women who had been term-limited out.

Another problem with the view that citizen legislators will be better representatives because their experiences gives them an understanding of constituents' interests is that political experience itself may give legislators a better understanding of constituents' interests. The experiences possessed by an individual citizen may not resemble experiences of others living in their same district. With large districts (over six hundred thousand residents), it is unlikely that someone living and working as a private citizen could understand the nature of the whole district, particularly a heterogeneous district. In *Federalist 56*, James Madison notes that experience in state legislatures helps members understand their states:

> The federal councils will derive great advantage from another circumstance. The representative of each state will not only bring with them considerable knowledge of its laws, and a local knowledge of their respective districts; but will probably in all cases have been members, and may even at the very time be members of the state legislature, where all the local information and interests of the state are assembled, and from whence they may easily be conveyed by a very few hands into the legislature of the United States (293).

A related reason offered as to why coming from the private sector is preferred is that political experience alters people. Often it is argued that professional legislators are so distant, physically and mentally, from constituents that they do not know what it is like to live under the laws they create. Consequently, they don't know the real needs and concerns of the citizenry. Additionally, they can become a ruling elite who come to expect privileges and are open to corruption. According to Fund (1992, 236), "It is a common observation that the longer a legislator works in Washington, D.C., or in a state capital, the more self-important that person seems to become. . . . In a capital city one is surrounded by individuals whose daily routine involves setting rules and regulations for the rest of society—a kind of 'culture of ruling.'" There are two problems with this argument. First, there is no evidence that long serving lawmakers fail to understand the needs of their districts. Reps. John Dingell (D-MI) and Frank Wolf (R-VA), two long serving members in the House, cannot be accused of becoming alienated from their districts' concerns. Second, as noted above, political experience may increase politicians' understanding of their district. By representing a district they meet a wide range of individuals and come to understand varied experiences.

Good representatives need to be ethical, and political careers are thought to offer opportunities for individuals to take advantage of the system for their personal gain. Even politicians with experience at lower levels are likely to be caught up in the trappings of the office and come to expect special treatment. Writing of state legislators, Rosenthal (1996, 32) states: "Because of the intense nature of their work and the fact that they are constantly at risk, a sense of power and entitlement develops among members of a legislative body to which legislators become susceptible." Prospective citizen legislators with their limited future career may be more ethical. Having limited careers may decrease the desire special interests or others will have to gain favor with members. Thus, citizen legislators with their short political careers are often expected to lack the time in office and political power that encourages unethical behavior. However, there is no research to support this view, while there is some that suggests career length has little effect on ethical behavior (Herrick 2003).

Not only is there little evidence that political experience per se causes unethical behavior, but there are reasons to predict that experience in the private sector may increase ethical problems, particularly conflict of interests. Retrospective citizen legislators who come from the private sector and prospective citizen legislators who plan to return quickly to the private sector are likely to have personal interests in the real world that can bias their decisions. For example, the only way for members who are farmers, and who continue to farm, to avoid voting on laws likely to affect agriculture is to not participate in debates on agriculture policy. However, when members do not participate in debates, they deny their constituents representation on the issue. In addition, members coming from the private sector are likely to have ties to private industry that could cause conflicts. For example, Vice-President Richard Cheney's ties with the Halliburton Company have caused the perception that the government granting Halliburton contracts to rebuild Iraq was inappropriate (Follman 2003). Another potential ethical concern relates to members' ties with interest groups. Retrospective citizen legislators with their lack of experience may become dependent on interest groups for information and services, because they have less familiarity with the legislative process or issues. Additionally, political experience may increase members' understanding of why some behaviors that are considered ethical in the private sector may not be ethical in the public sector.

The second issue concerning the value of private versus political experience is whether political experience increases political effectiveness. Members who have previous political experience should be effective early on in their House careers because they are more likely to understand the issues and the legislative/political process, and they have increased chances hold leadership positions (Louison 1988, Berkman 1993, and Boulard 1994).

Although prospective citizen legislators will not have less experience while they are in office, their lack of a future political career too may affect their ability to represent their constituents. Other members may know that prospective citizen legislators will not be around long, and thus they may be reluctant to invest time in working with citizen legislators. In a sense, they arrive as lame-ducks with the consequence of a weaker bargaining position in relation to their colleagues. They cannot make deals that involve future behavior. Other members may be reluctant to work on building working relationships with those they know will not be around very long; such work would only have short term benefits. Additionally, party leaders may be less likely to give them key committee assignments since they are in a position to be less responsive to the leadership.

The last issue concerns whether political ambition helps or hinders the ability of members to represent their constituents. Political ambition is the desire to have a political career, regardless of motivations behind that desire. Schlesinger (1966) identified three types of ambition: 1) static ambition, the desire for the current position; 2) discrete ambition, the desire to leave politics; and 3) progressive ambition, the desire for a higher office. To these, others have added intra-institutional ambition, the desire for a leadership position in one's current chamber (Herrick and Moore 1993). Generally, the research on ambition has tended to treat each type as nominal level data; either you have the ambition or you do not. With this work, we tend to conceptualize ambition as more of a continuum. Our citizen legislators do not lack ambition, but just have lower grades of ambition than professional politicians. Clearly prospective citizen legislators have less static and progressive ambition than prospective professional legislators but more discrete ambition. However, retrospective citizen legislators may also have more discrete ambition than experienced politicians, because they have private sector careers to which they can return. According to Rep. Bill McCollum (R-FL),

> Because what has happened is that since the days of our Founding Fathers, we have become a full-time year-around Congress. Instead of having Members like they did in the old days come here and only serve two months out of the year, they serve the whole year, they have to give up jobs, we are not allowed to have professions any longer, so on and so forth, no outside earning for most Members. The institution creates a congressional career orientation. Naturally there is a tendency on the part of many to want to stay here and to get reelected because they do not have a job to go back to back home (*Congressional Record* 1995, H3937).

Our main concern is with discrete ambition. What are the behaviors of those who do not want a future, or a long future, in politics? There are three ways discrete ambition may affect representation: what members do when they leave office, motivations for office, and the value of reelection.

First, it is feared that members with discrete ambition will spend their last years in office working to obtain lucrative post-congressional careers such as lobbying for a firm (Cain 1994, 47). During House debate on term limits Rep. Marge Roukema (R-NJ) stated that term limits "only exacerbate the so-called revolving door syndrome, elected officials spending their time and energy while in office paving the way for a lucrative job in the private sector with the special-interest groups they have been serving after they leave office. Automatic term limits will intensify and institutionalize the resume-building that already occurs all too often in this Congress" (*Congressional Record* 1995, H3898).

Second, ambition may be related to motives for wanting a political position. For example, the Citizens for Term Limits's web page states:

> Term limits will accomplish a number of positive things, but one stands out; it will improve the quality of leadership of our congressional public servants by a quantum amount, by replacing careerists whose primary motives are reelection, with citizen legislators whose motives are to serve the country (www.termlimits.com/position.htm).

This argument, which applies primarily to prospective citizen legislators, suggests that the key motivational difference expected between citizen and professional legislators is that citizen legislators are more policy oriented and less career oriented. Some support for this expectation has been found. Herrick and Thomas (2005) compared the motivations state legislators gave for wanting to hold office who were elected where and when term limits were in effect with the motivations[7] of legislators elected without term limits. They found term-limited legislators were more likely to report that they were motivated to serve out of a desire to affect policy than were non-term-limited legislators. However, the research on motivations does not suggest policy motives lead to greater or better representation.

First, the research generally finds that members with policy motives are ideologues who are not willing to compromise (Costantini and Valenty 1996) and less likely to support their parties (Fishel 1971).[8] Also, Payne (1984) believes politicians motivated by policy goals are just as self-serving as those motivated to attaining power and status; both are fulfilling an emotional need. This discussion of motivations does not lead one to expect that citizen legislators will necessarily be more representative of their constituents. If they are policy motivated, they are likely to work on those policies regardless of constituents' interests. If the legislators' policy concerns overlap with the voters it could be argued that there would be strong substantive representation. However, this view has a weakness. When policy interests do not overlap, constituents' wishes are likely to be ignored. In this case, they may be represented by members who are uncompromisingly working for policies that are not in the their best interest.

Political ambition is also thought to affect behavior, because it will affect the importance of reelection to members. Although it can be assumed members with discrete ambition are likely to be less reelection-focused, it is uncertain whether being free from elections improves or harms members' ability to represent their constituents' interests. On one hand, it has been argued that elections lead to superficial behaviors by incumbents instead of quality policy making. For example, Mayhew (1974) examined Congress based on the assumption that members were only interested in reelection and concluded that instead of spending time legislating, members spend time advertising themselves, taking positions and taking credit for good things that happen. A related issue is the perception that professional legislators are so tied to special interest groups that they represent these interests instead of their constituents' interests. Members focused on reelection need campaign money, much of which comes from political action committees (PACs). Fiorina (1989) suggests that to get reelected, members spend significant time passing pork-barrel legislation and increasing government regulation as a means to aid constituents. Bickers and Stein (1996) also find that members who are electorally insecure bring more pork back to the district than more secure members. Similarly, Carey, Niemi, and Powell (2000) found that state legislators from term-limited states (who have limited static ambition) were less active in pork-barreling than those from non-term-limited states. However, less pork-barreling does not translate to more representation. Since constituents benefit from and want pork brought to their districts, such behavior can be seen as a type of representation (Weisberg, Heberling, and Campoli 1999, 75).

On the other hand, freedom from the desire to be reelected may harm representation. According to James Madison, "As it is essential to liberty, that the government in general should have a common interest with the people; so it is particularly essential that the branch of it under consideration should have an immediate dependence on, and an intimate sympathy with, the people. Frequent elections are unquestionably the only policy, by which this dependence and sympathy can be effectually secured" (2001, 273). Although most term limits supporters argue less political ambition increases responsiveness, some have argued that legislators free from electoral constraints will be less responsive. During debates on term limits Rep. Henry Hyde (R-IL) noted the conflicting arguments for term limits, "There are two contradictory arguments which support term-limits issue. One is that we are too focused on reelection, not close enough to the people. Then you have the George Will theory that we are too close to the people, too responsive, and we need a constitutional distance from them" (*Congressional Record* 1995, H3905).[9]

Members who want to stay in office need to be sensitive to voters or they will not win reelection. Prospective citizen legislators have less incentive to be attentive to constituents since they have less interest in reelection than professional politicians. In other words, elections, and the prospect of losing a reelection bid, constrain members. Some of the research on congressional retirement supports such beliefs. In the Congress prior to members' retirement, members' attendance fell off (Lott 1990; Herrick, Moore, and Hibbing 1994); they were generally less active, including making fewer trips back to the district (Herrick, Moore, and Hibbing 1994), and they altered their voting behavior (Zupan 1990; Carey 1994; Rothenberg and Sanders 2000). Evidence from state legislatures with term limits also suggests that term-limited members spend less time contacting constituents (Carey, Niemi, and Powell 2000).

Congressional critics have an additional point about elections. Ambitious politicians are not constrained by elections because of the incumbency advantage. Because incumbents are virtually assured reelection, they can effectively ignore their constituents and still be reelected. Whether this happens is debatable. Jacobson (1987) notes that members of Congress run scared, worrying about losing their reelection. The extensive amount of time and effort devoted to fund-raising between election campaigns is testament to that. Even if members were not concerned about their reelection, the argument would be that there is no difference between citizen and professional legislators in how they represent their constituents.

The above debates relate differently for our different types of citizen legislators. The debate concerning private versus political experience relates more to retrospective citizen legislators than prospective, but not exclusively. The debates concerning the value of ambition and reelections relate more to be prospective legislators than to retrospective citizen legislators, but not exclusively. We generally find the arguments suggest citizen legislators, of either variety, to be either weaker representatives or not to differ significantly from professional legislators.

The Data

This book examines whether citizen and professional legislators offer their constituents a different quality of representation. To do so, we examine House members elected to Congress between 1992-1998. This period was selected since it corresponds to the time period of the greatest outcry against professional legislators and the greatest push for citizen legislators. From this group of House members, we delete members who had previously served in the House. This gives us an initial population of 321 members.

For most of the analyses we examine the first two congresses of behavior. Two congresses were used since members who entered planning to have a short career and changed their minds would be less likely to have made the decision to violate their pledge this early. Thus they would still be behaving like those with short-term ambition. Additionally, we feared that just looking at the first congress would be too short of a period of time. With these analyses we did not include members who won special elections or left during their second term. Since their length of service was different than members who had two full terms, their roll-call votes or other behaviors would be based on a shorter period. This time period reflects our assumption that while career decisions can change, they are unlikely to do so too quickly. This left us with 271 members.

To determine which members were prospective citizen legislators, we relied on an indirect measure of members' career goals. Direct measures would unlikely yield meaningful data. Members are unlikely to respond to questionnaires and even if they did they would likely give socially desirable answers to questions about their career plans. Instead we tend to measure behaviors that indicate desires. Our measure is whether members signed and kept the term limits pledge circulated by the U.S. Term Limits organization. There were twenty-eight members who signed and kept the term limit pledge.

A concern with using voluntary pledges is that the pledge may be given for political reasons with no intention of following through with it, and members are at some level free to violate the pledge. However, we do not see this as a significant problem since the pledge was signed and kept. We believe their signatures increased members' commitment to follow the pledge. For this reason, we did not use statements made during a campaign but only the signed pledge as an indication of a limited term. Additionally, we only included members who kept their pledge gives us greater confidence in the validity of the measure. Because we were skeptical that prospective citizen legislators would differ dramatically from prospective professional legislators, we wanted to make sure that only truly progressive citizen legislators were coded as such. Since few members are prospective citizen legislators, we wanted to make sure that only citizen legislators were included because a few outliers could have great effects. We acknowledge that we may have coded a few members incorrectly. However, had we included members who broke the pledge, we would have included members who should not have been coded as progressive citizen legislators.[10] We are interested in the effects of long-term political career goals, not just static ambition. Members who signed the pledge could, and many did, run for higher office at the end of their term. However, we assume that these members were sincere in their desire to have a limited congressional career when they entered office. ANOVA is used to examine differences between prospective citizen legislators operational-ized as all who signed and kept the pledge and those who did not seek a higher office. See Appendix B for a table of the different means. A discussion of what the table indicates about the findings is offered as an end note in each chapter.

Some readers may wonder why we did not examine state legislators, since there are legal term limits at the state level and more members with little or no previous experience. We believe there is much value to examining the case of the U.S. Congress. The debate over what constitutes a good representative has been focused at the national level. Since state legislators do not have to leave their communities to the same degree that U.S. Congress members do, they are less likely to lose touch with the district. Although there is considerable varia-tion in the professionalism of state legislatures, few state legislators have the types of pressures and expectations placed on them as do House members. Thus the difference between citizen and professional legislators is likely greater in the House than in state assemblies. Additionally, the data we needed to examine the different aspects of representation are not uniformly available across states. Even if these data were available, the context of the states could affect the types of representation expected of their state legislators. Thus comparisons would be problematic. Additionally, the fact that the pledge is voluntary is an advantage since we are interested in citizen legislators not the effects of term limits per se.[11] If we compared legislators who had legislative term limits with those who did not, we would be more likely to include legislators who never intended to have a limited political career but who saw a term-limited office as a first step-ping stone to higher office. While we acknowledge that some of our members who signed the pledge used it as a political tool, we are likely to have fewer such members who do not want a political career than we would if we used legal term limits as the indicator of members who plan to stay in the House a short period of time.

To estimate which of our members were retrospective citizen legislators, we determined who came to the House without previous political experience. To do this we rely on biographies of freshmen printed in *CQ's Weekly Report* (various years) and Clerk of the House's members' biographies. If any previous political experience, other than running for an office they did not win or holding a party office or working for an interest group,[12] was listed in the members' biography then we coded that member has having previous political experience. The types of offices include state legislators, assorted state level elective offices, legisla-tive or executive[13] staff, commissioners, city and county councils, mayors, sher-iffs, prosecutors or judges, and school board members or superintendents. Most of the research that has examined the effects of political experience on mem-bers' behavior focused on state legislative experience. We chose to use any po-litical experience as the defining characteristic. Any political experience is likely to have some effects similar to that of a state legislator. Many positions besides state legislator, e.g., mayor or city council, likely give people feelings of entitlement and distance them from average citizens, increase their understanding of the larger community, and involve collective decision making and an understanding of politics. We do not include positions that are outside of the government, such as lobbyist or party official. They do not have the same prestige, or relationship with constituents that could give a large understanding of the community nor do they involve the same type of collective decision making.

Since the key with retrospective professional legislators is that they saw politics as their main career prior to entering the House, we needed to consider how long members had served in politics. Looking at number of years was problematic since members differ in their ages. Thus we took the number of years members served in politics as a percentage of the member's life after the age of twenty-five. Twenty-five was used since it was the youngest a member could be to enter the House. Because a large number of members had no prior experience we treat the data as a dichotomy. To do this we need to determine what percentage of time a member had to have previously held a political post. More than 50 percent seemed too large of a percentage since it often takes time to develop skills and contacts to run successfully for office or to wait for an open seat. We chose 33 percent as the cut off. In part this was chosen because it was a common fraction and in part because it was a nice dividing line. About 25 percent of those with some political experience were coded as not having retrospective political careers with this cut off.

We use ordinary least squares regression or logistic regression, depending on the nature of the dependent variable, to examine the differences between citizen and professional legislators. Since there was not a strong correlation ($r=.14$; $p=.01$) between retrospective and prospective citizen legislators, we include both in the equations. Unless otherwise noted, in these analyses we control for when the member entered with a series of dummy variables. There was a variable for those entering in the 103rd Congress, one for those entering in the 104th Congress, and another for those entering in the 105th Congress. The 106th congressional class served as the reference group. We control for when members entered the House since the frequency of the election of retrospective and prospective citizen legislators varied over time. Also, conditions likely to affect the dependent variables varied over time. A second common control was party identification. As will be discussed in the next chapter, citizen legislators are more likely to be Republican and party identification affects numerous political behaviors. Since we examine a population and not a sample, we know the differences did not occur because of sampling error, and measures of statistical significance technically are of limited value. But we do see them as having some value in indicating the relative value of a relationship and thus report them. Additionally, it should be noted that we examined correlations for any indication that multicollinearity was a problem, and where it is an issue we discuss it.

To supplement the above analysis we made a more in-depth examination of seven members. Of the seven members, four signed the term limit pledge. Bob Riley, a Republican from Alabama who is now governor of the state, served from 1997-2002. He also served in the Ashland City Council from 1972-1976. Tillie Fowler, a Republican from Florida, passed away in 2005, but had been working for a major law firm in D.C. at the time of her death. She served in the House from 1993-2000 and had served on the Jacksonville City Council from 1985-1992. Tom Coburn, a Republican from Oklahoma, won a U.S. Senate seat in 2004. He served in the House from 1995-2000 and had no prior political experience. Mark Sanford, a Republican from South Carolina, is currently governor of South Carolina. He served from 1995-2000 and also had no prior political experience. Three members did not sign the pledge and had different types of previous political experience. They were Frank Lucas, a Republican from Oklahoma, Tom Allen, a Democrat from Maine, and Sue Kelly, a Republican from New York. Kelly was first elected in 1994. She had served as a legislative aide in the House for Rep. Hamilton Fish. Lucas was elected to the House in 1994 and had served in the Oklahoma House (1988-1994). Allen was elected to the House in 1997 and had served as mayor to Portland prior and had been in the city council from 1989-1995. These members were selected with an eye toward having a sample of House members with and without the characteristics of citizen legislators who were comparable while still allowing for some diversity in gender, party, and region of the country. These members also vary considerably in the types of previous life experience. To examine these members we read news accounts in the *Washington Post* and *CQ Weekly Report*, conducted interviews with some of them and with a few staffers, and read other accounts of the members' experiences, such as books written by members. The interviews of congressional staff and members were semi-structured and lasted about thirty minutes each. These case studies added greater context and detail to what is found in the quantitative analysis.

In the rest of the book we empirically examine differences between citizen and professional legislators in how they represent their districts, keeping an eye on how the two different types of citizen legislators differ. Chapter Two examines whether citizen legislators or professional legislators offer more descriptive representation. It also indicates whether citizen legislators are more likely to know the interests of their constituents by having experiences similar to them. Chapter Three observes whether citizen or professional legislators more actively keep in touch with their districts. One sign of district commitment is whether citizen or professional legislators spend more energy on communicating with the district through the use of their franking privilege, the proportion of staff based in the district, and the frequency of trips to the district. Keeping in contact also offers members another way to know the interests of their constituents. Chapter Four covers "acting for" or substantive representation, examining whether citizen or professional legislators are more likely to vote consistently with the interests of their districts (e.g., members whose constituents voted Democratic should have a liberal voting record), and whether they are more ideological. To be quality representatives, members need to be active and effective policy makers. Chapter Five tests whether citizen or professional legislators introduce more legislation, are more likely to see that legislation pass, achieve key committee assignments, or are mentioned in the national press. Chapter Six explores whether accusations of unethical behavior or convictions for unethical behavior differ between the two groups. Another concern with the representation of professional legislators is that they become tied to special interests to the district's detriment. In Chapter Seven we examine members' connections to interest groups to estimate whether professional legislators have greater connections. Chapter Eight synthesizes our findings and offers a final assessment of how citizen and professional legislators differ in their representational styles.

Citizen legislators versus professional legislators conjures up images from Frank Capra's *Mr. Smith Goes to Washington*: the man with no political ambition is snapped up from the masses to go to Washington and represent the people only to run afoul of the professional politicians, elected and unelected, who seek to line their own pockets at the expense of those they represent. The debate in the 1990s over citizen legislators is the real life continuation of that 1930s drama. While supporters of citizen legislators view Mr. Smith's adversaries as ancestors of today's professional legislator, opponents argue Mr. Smith is a caricature, and that professional legislators are not inherently corrupt or unrepresentative. We hope to peel away the rhetoric on both sides of the argument to provide a more objective picture.

Notes

1. Citizen legislators could be defined as legislators who have both characteristics; however, because of a small number of members, an analysis of these is not possible. Also, the data will show that the two different characteristics can work at cross-purposes.

2. Pitkin (1967, 110) also identified authoritative and symbolic representation. With authoritative representation the representative has power based on formal relationships. With symbolic representation a person or object stands for something else by serving as a representation of it. Flags, for example, represent nations. The key with symbolic representation is that the people perceive the symbols as a genuine representation.

3. Pitkin (1967) suggests that pure trustee representation is not representation because the represented have to know their interests and trustees do not act as if they do. Also, pure delegate representation is not representation because the representative is not free to act.

4. The two other legislative principles are fairness (that the members play by the same rules and that the rules are fair) and accountability (that the members do not harm the public's esteem for the chamber).

5. Hastings Center uses the term autonomous, that "legislators have an obligation to deliberate and decide, free from improper influence" (1985, 34), to mean essentially the same as independence.

6. Another expectation of instituting term limit law is that it will increase the competitiveness of elections so that more people will seek and win office; and that different kinds of people will seek and win office (Jacob 1994, 41-42; Petracca 1992, 74-75; Allebaugh and Pinney 2003; Armor 1994). Term limits laws are expected to increase competition since they will diminish the incumbency advantage. Since the vast majority of in-

cumbents win, if incumbents cannot seek reelection, there will be more open seats and consequently more competition. By increasing competition the presence of term limits may change the composition of Congress. For example, it is often argued that few women are in Congress because incumbents are predominately male and are highly likely to win reelection. Thus, if incumbents cannot seek reelection, then there are more opportunities for women to win seats. The argument that term limit laws will change the composition of Congress is of little relevance to this study since it requires a structural change that will not occur without legally binding limits on most members. It does not suggest that citizen legislators elected at one point in time will offer more descriptive representation than professional legislators elected at the same time. Nevertheless, if citizen legislators are expected to better represent the people because they have similar experiences as their constituents, then they need to be similar to their constituents in demographic characteristics.

7. The literature on career motivation does not clearly define motivation (Lasswell 1974; Browning and Jacob 1964; Payne 1984; Costantini 1990; Costantini and Valenty 1996). To Lasswell and Browning and Jacob motivations relate to personality types, to Payne they are emotional needs satisfied by holding office, and to Costantini and Valenty they are simply the reasons for becoming politically active. The key difference between the definitions relates to the origins of the motives, but generally the idea is that people seek office to fulfill some need. Ultimately individuals gain something personally from serving.

8. Fishel (1971, 33) used the term careerism, which was based on "subjective factors" that measure "career commitment." Costantini and Valenty (1996) used the term ambition, which is the person wanting a political career.

9. There is a conflict within the term limits movement about the role of elections. To some term limits supporters, term limits are needed to make the members closer to the people. Terms may accomplish this by limiting members' need to respond to interest group demands. The other view is that term limits will free members from having to cater to the narrow shortsighted self-interests of the voters.

10. We ran the analyses using all who signed the pledge as the measure of prospective citizen legislators. Where the findings differed from the measure used, changed direction or became/failed to be statistically significant, we report that in footnotes.

11. A few states did pass term limit laws for their U.S. Congress members which were later deemed unconstitutional by the courts (*U.S. Term Limits, Inc. v. Thornton* 1995 (115 S. Ct. 1842)). A handful of members in our data set were elected the year their state voted for term limits and were consequently not affected by the term limits. Another handful of members from states with federal term limits legislation came to office the year term limits were declared unconstitutional. These members and candidates knew the courts were reviewing the Arkansas law when they ran and served fewer than six months believing there was a chance their term would be limited. Only one member, Scott McInnis (R-CO), served a whole term with his term limited.

12. We did not code members whose only previous experience was a party position as having previous political experience. Although this is a valuable experience it does not require facing the voters, making decisions in a legislative body, nor does it have the same access to perks of office.

13. Executive staff includes working for either the state or the federal executive branches.

Chapter Two
Descriptive Representation

Since professional legislators lack the everyday experiences of average Americans, they are presumed to be distant and out of touch with their constituents. On the other hand citizen legislators, who are thought to have the everyday experiences of average Americans, are presumed to understand the lives of constituents, working a job, paying taxes, living with government regulations, and being present in the community. Arguments that citizen legislators' private lives give them an understanding of average Americans presuppose that they have meaningful shared experiences. For this to be the case, they would have to be similar to Americans in critical socio-demographic characteristics. Individuals' characteristics shape their experiences. Women's experiences differ from men, blacks from whites or Latinos, wealthy from poor, and so on. Thus, citizen legislators would need to offer more descriptive representation.

Mansbridge (1999) suggests there are two ways descriptive representation can be achieved.[1] One way is through the random selection of members. A lottery or similar mode of randomization could be used to select members. The other way is to have an electoral system that insures people with certain characteristics are elected. For example, in the United States, the fact that House members represent districts within states helps insure a roughly geographically proportional legislature. Also, since the 1980s, majority-minority districts have been created during the redistricting process for the House of Representatives with the goal of increasing the number of racial and ethnic minority representatives. In addition, descriptive representation could be enhanced, although unlikely to be fully achieved, by having a political system that encourages average citizens to run for office and, furthermore, encourages voters to support such candidates. It is in this latter way that the citizen legislator movement of the 1990s may help enhance descriptive representation. If the average citizen is upset with the entrenched professional legislator, and there is a viable alternative, such as a citizen legislative candidate, then there should be greater descriptive representation.[2]

To estimate whether a citizen legislature offers more descriptive representation than a professional legislature it is necessary to identify "the people" or constituency. There are two general conceptualizations of constituents: a district constituency or a national constituency. Although district constituency seem the most appropriate with the U.S. electoral system, both of these constituencies have some validity, and we will examine both. The structure of U.S. House districts primarily insures the former. But, the notion of descriptive representation focuses more on the latter. It is not that an individual member should look like all of America; rather the whole legislature should mirror the economic, racial, ethnic, and religious diversity of America. Consequently, the pool of citizen legislators should better resemble America than the pool of professional legislators.

The other way to conceptualize the people or constituency is based on the individuals living in a member's district. Fenno (1977) termed this the geographic constituency. When members speak about their constituency they are typically referring to their geographic constituency. Additionally, much of the research examining substantive representation focuses on the degree to which members act on behalf of this constituency, not the national constituency. For example, many researchers have examined whether members' roll-call votes mirrored the opinions of the district not the nation (see for example Miller and Stokes 1963; Holian, Krebs, and Walsh 1997; Gartzke and Wrighton 1998). It is also consistent with the structure of Congressional elections as members are selected through district elections. With this conceptualization, if citizen legislators provide more descriptive representation than professional legislators do, it is a consequence of having a better resemblance to the individuals living in the districts they serve. A citizen legislator may not share all the descriptive characteristics of district constituents, but they should more closely match those characteristics than professional legislators.

What are the key characteristics of the people that the legislative body should reflect? As Pitkin (1967, 77) noted, "Not many people, after all, seriously think that the best legislator is one who is typical and average in every conceivable respect, including, intelligence, public spiritedness, and experience." Although some advocates of citizen legislators come close to advocating for typical or average legislators, we argue that the key characteristics are those that are politically relevant which are those that differentiate individuals' political positions. Other important characteristics are those shared by people who have a history of being left out of the political system, such as women and racial minorities. These people need to be included for the system to be fair, and for all Americans to see the process as legitimate. Mansbridge (1999, 652) writes, "voters and designers of representative institutions should accept some of the costs of descriptive representation in historical circumstances when (1) communication is impaired, often by mistrust; (2) interests are relatively uncrystallized; (3) a group has once been considered unfit to rule; and (4) de facto legitimacy is low within the group." In these situations, having representatives of the key groups can help insure voices are heard, and, as a consequence, it legitimizes the process.

Do Citizen Legislators Offer Greater Descriptive Representation?

The main reason that citizen legislators would differ from professional legislators in their socio-demographic characteristics would be that ambition is related to these characteristics. That is, members who want shorter careers, but still want a career, would not have the same characteristics as others. Two factors affect whether someone runs for a political position: ambition and opportunity for gaining the political position. We believe that both of these factors suggest that average Americans are not likely to run for or win office.

First, Americans from a variety of backgrounds may not want to serve in Congress. Research on women in Congress illustrates this point. Although recent research suggests women politicians are similar to male politicians in their ambition, women in the general population have less political ambition than men. Constantini (1990), who examined the political ambition of women from 1964-1984, found the gap shrinking, but women still have less desire than men for a political career. More recently the Citizen Political Ambition Study found that women who are in a pool of eligible candidates are less likely to have considered running for office than similar men (Fox and Lawless 2004). Also, since women are usually primary caregivers of their children, they tend to enter politics later in life and are less likely to have the long professional career that men have (Herrick 2004). Additionally, research indicates that women are more likely to run for office if they have a supportive family, but for men this is not an important factor (Dodson 1997; Carroll 1989; Thomas, Herrick and Braunstein 2003). Other research too suggests that people likely to enter politics will not be evenly distributed. Assuming interest in politics generally is needed to run for office, people with lower socio-economic status, some ethnic groups, and women should be less likely to run since they are less likely to be interested in politics (Conway, Stavernagel, and Ahern 1997).

Even if average Americans had the desire to run for office, they are unlikely to be considered viable candidates. Enormous resources are needed to win elections, resources most Americans lack. Because of the hurdles inherent to running for office, it might be expected that more Americans would be willing to serve than would choose to run. It takes contacts and money, major stumbling blocks for many people. In the 2004 elections, the average Democratic open-seat House candidate raised $935,296 and the average Republican open-seat candidate raised $1,352,598 (http://www.FEC.gov/press/press2004/ 20050103canstat/ medianhousepost2004.pdf). With the current system there are two ways to finance campaigns: ask others for money or spend your own money. Candidates can and do spend their own money on their elections, but such candidates could not be termed average Americans. Candidates can raise money through donations from wealthy individuals and political action committees (PACs). However, this requires extensive contacts. PACs and other donors also tend to give to viable candidates. Smart political operators do not give significant amounts of money to just anyone. It is unlikely that the average American has the contacts needed to raise the amount of money needed. Nor is it likely that the average

American will be able to project herself or himself as a credible candidate in very many races.

An additional hurdle for average Americans wanting to serve in Congress is that to get elected there must be a constituency interested in and willing to vote for such candidates. It is unclear whether voters are likely to elect citizen legislators. Although they support term limits and distrust the Congress, they also reelect and love their own members. Although Americans are more likely to vote for women and racial minorities today than in the past, there remain some Americans who prefer white male legislators. For example, in a 1991 national survey, 9 percent of the respondents said they would not vote for a woman for president of their party if she was qualified (Darcy, Welch, and Clark 1994, 176). Also in recent years 90-95 percent of Americans say they would vote for black candidate for president (Bardes and Oldendick 2003, 172-74). This means 5 percent to 10 percent may not vote for a black candidate. These polling data likely undercount the percentage of Americans unwilling to vote for women and minorities, because these types of questions likely generate socially desirable responses. Most Americans also prefer successful and attractive candidates, not average Americans. Americans elect candidates with political experience, who are successful and attractive. Research on voters' prototypical president finds that voters want someone who is not typical. They want presidents who are honest, knowledgeable, open minded, and courageous (Kinder et al. 1980) as well as having high levels of competence, integrity, reliability, and charisma (Miller, Wattenberg, and Malanchuk 1986). There is some evidence too that voters want legislators who have high levels of instrumentality: assertive, coarse, tough, aggressive, stern, masculine, active, rational, and confident (Huddy and Terkeldsen 1993). As a result, candidates lacking these characteristics, especially those associated with masculinity, are at a disadvantage.

National Constituency

To test whether citizen legislators better mirror America than professional legislators, we compare the demographic characteristics of retrospective and prospective citizen legislators with professional legislators. The characteristics we used for the comparisons include party, education, income, gender, race, age, and occupation. Americans who differ on these characteristics differ on key political issues. Another reason for examining these characteristics is that members of Congress do not reflect the general population on these characteristics. Although members do not differ dramatically from the general population in party,[3] they generally are richer and have higher social status and are more likely to be male, white, and older than the general population. If prospective citizen legislators offer greater descriptive representation than prospective professional legislators, then the mean of this group should be more like the voters' mean. Similar expectations are held for retrospective citizen compared to retrospective professional legislators. Also, since America is a diverse nation, if prospective and retrospective citizen legislators offer greater descriptive representation, then the diversity of these groups should likewise be larger than that of other members. Therefore, we also examine the standard deviations of the different types of legislators to see if citizen legislators are more diverse as a group than are professional legislators.

We examine legislators' wealth and education, because each is related to party identification, issue positions, and ideology (Erikson and Tedin 2001, 205; Hershey and Beck 2003, 131). Additionally, if part of the reason citizen legislators are expected to differ from professional legislators is that they have similar experiences, which gives them a better understanding of what it is like to live under the rules they create, then wealth and education are important since they affect these experiences. Better educated, and wealthier Americans undoubtedly have access to more resources. Wealth and education were measured by the member's level of education and income. Each member's education was coded using the following scheme: graduate education is four, college degree is three, high school diploma is two, and less than a high school education is one. These data came from CQ's biographies of freshmen members of Congress.

Estimates of members' incomes were calculated from members' financial disclosure statements filed in their first congress. We used members' first financial disclosure statements, and totaled their earned and unearned income and standardized it in 1999 dollars.[4] We did not calculate income for members entering the House by a special election since they did not have a full year of non-House income to list. Determining an individual member's earned and unearned income was not as straightforward as it might seem. While members are required to disclose their income sources, they do not provide a specific dollar figure for each source but only a category for each source. For example, a member would list a specific income source and then specify whether it was valued between $0-1,000; $1,001-15,000; $15,001-50,000; $50,001-100,000; $100,001-250,000, $250,001-500,000; $500,001-1,000,000; $1,000,001-5,000,000; and so on. Following Stewart (1994), we used the middle dollar figure for each category to estimate the value of the individual source. Since the data collected covered a six-year period, and American salaries and the cost of living increased during that time period, each member's income was standardized using 1999 dollars.[5]

We also examined occupational differences. The key occupational difference was whether citizen legislators were less likely to be lawyers than were professional legislators. Historically, the number of lawyers in Congress has been disproportionately large, which means that citizens of other professions are underrepresented. There are negative feelings about this large number of lawyers in Congress. Members who were listed as lawyers or as having law degrees in CQ's Freshmen Biographies were coded one and other members were coded zero.

Third, differences in gender were examined. Since the 1980s, researchers have noted a gender gap in political attitudes and voting behavior. Women are generally more liberal than men and differ in their support for some key policies, political party identification, and support for individual politicians (see Andersen 1997 for a discussion of the literature). Gender was coded such that women were coded one and men coded zero.

A fourth demographic classification we examined was race. Individuals of different races tend to differ in key political beliefs and voting behavior (Rosenstone and Hansen 1993). Again, we would expect citizen legislators, if they are closer to the American people in demographic characteristics, to be more racially diverse than professional legislators. Race was coded such that whites were coded one and nonwhites coded zero.[6]

Fifth, we examined differences in age. There are two main theories that predict that an individual's age is related to his/her political values and attitudes. Generational theory suggests that individuals of an age cohort have similar socializing forces that can affect their perceptions and attitudes (for example, see Jennings and Niemi 1974; Kertzer 1983; Kornberg and Thomas 1965; Delli Carpini 1986). People whose political views were shaped during the same historical period have similar forces affecting their political development. For example, those who come of age during periods of economic hardship have different views of money than those who come of age during periods of economic growth. On the other hand, life-cycles theory predicts that maturation affects people's political attitudes (Conway 1991, 17-18). For example, older people may be expected to be more concerned with maintaining social security than with student loans. Thus, if the pool of retrospective and the pool of prospective citizen legislators of the 1990s resemble America, then as a group they should be nearer the average age of Americans. Members' ages were calculated by subtracting the year in which members were born, as reported in *CQ*'s biographies of freshmen, from the year they entered.

Sixth, political party affiliation was examined. Since the *American Voter* (Campbell et al. 1960), party identification has been considered politically relevant. It is related to citizens' social status and family background, which in turn influences political opinions and electoral behavior, as well as to elite opinions and behavior.[7] Again, if citizen legislators are similar to Americans, we expect their party breakdown to be fairly similar. Although many Americans identify as independents or nonpartisans, if we assume they are fairly evenly split between the parties, then the proportions of Democrats and Republicans should be fairly similar. Of course, this depends on the survey and the time period. Democrats were coded one and Republicans coded zero.

Findings

The dependent variable is the type of legislator. The expectation is that certain types of people are more likely to be citizen as opposed to professional legislators, or have different types of political ambition. Table 2.1 reports the logistic regression equations that estimate the degree to which age, income, education, party affiliation, race (white), and occupation (whether they practice law) pre-

Table 2.1. Demographic Differences Between Citizen and Professional Legislators: National Constituency

	Prospective	Retrospective
Education	.73*	.33+
	(.39)	(.23)
Income	.0003	.001**
	(.0005)	(.0005)
Law	-1.04*	-.33
	(.54)	(.32)
Race (white)	6.17	.27
	(16.19)	(.42)
Gender (female)	.15	.81**
	(.69)	(.36)
Age	.0004	.003
	(.0274)	(.017)
Party (Democrat)	-1.38**	-.76***
	(.59)	(.29)
103rd Congress	-.56	.55+
	(.71)	(.44)
104th Congress	.0004	.72*
	(.65)	(.44)
105th Congress	-.25	.56
	(.73)	(.45)
Constant	-10.05	-2.08*
	(16.30)	(1.20)
Cox and Snell R^2	.08	.08
Nagelkerke R^2	.16	.11
N	292	292
Chi^2	22.82**	25.45***

+< .20 * < .10 ** <.05 *** < .01 (using a two-tailed test)

Sources: *CQ's Biographies of Freshman Members* (various years), *CQ Politics in America*, www. Bioguide.congress.gov/biosearch/biosearch.asp, and *Financial Disclosure Reports of House Members* (various Congresses). Data calculated by authors. See Appendix A for explanation of the variables.

dicts if a member is a citizen or professional legislator. According to Table 2.1 prospective citizen legislators were not more similar to the American population than were professional legislators. With the exception of party, positive coefficients indicate that prospective citizen legislators were more elite and most of the coefficients were positive.[8] The relationship for education was statistically significant. Whereas the average member had a .19 probability of being a prospective citizen legislator, one that scored one standard deviation below the mean had a .10 probability.[9] There were two significant negative relationships. One was for party. While the average Republican had a .19 probability of being a prospective citizen legislator the average Democrat had a .06 probability. This indicates they were more likely to be Republican rather than a similarity to average Americans. The other negative relationship is for occupation. Lawyers were less likely to be prospective citizen legislators than professional legislators. The average non-lawyer had a .19 probability of being a citizen legislator and the average lawyer had a .08 probability of being a prospective citizen legislator. The fact that they were less likely to be lawyers may indicate that these members differ in ambition since law is a common road to politics (Fox and Lawless 2004).

Members more similar to average Americans were not more likely to be retrospective citizen legislators than retrospective professional legislators either. Higher levels of education and income were associated with being a citizen not a professional legislator. The average member had a .50 probability of being a retrospective citizen legislator whereas one scoring above the mean in income had a .59 probability and one scoring a standard deviation below the mean in education a .42 probability. These differences at least neared statistical significance. Citizen legislators were also significantly more likely to be Republican. There was one minority group more likely to be citizen than professional legislators—women. Women had a .69 probability of being retrospective citizen legislators. Men had a .50 probability.

It should also be noted that all categories of legislators had incomes highly in excess of the national median household income: in 2000 it was about $42,000 (http://www.census.gov/prod.cen2000/dp1/2kh00.pdf). Of the different types of legislators it is the average retrospective professional legislator that had the smallest income of about $145,000. Legislators of all types of ambition also were much better educated than the average American, since both types of legislators had at least a college degree. Based on the 2000 Census, only 24.4 percent of Americans have at least a college degree.

Not only do the findings suggest that the average prospective citizen legislator was not more similar to the average American than the average professional legislator, but they also suggest that citizen legislators were not a more heterogeneous group. An examination of the standard deviations (not reported) does not show a pattern of prospective citizen legislators being more diverse than other members. If anything, they were less diverse. They had smaller standard deviations in income, party, gender, race, and having a law degree, and only had larger standard deviations in age. Retrospective citizen legislators were slightly more diverse than retrospective professional legislators. They had larger standard deviations with regard to education, income, age, and gender.

To this point, the findings offer little evidence that citizen legislators were more similar to the average American than were professional legislators. In fact the evidence generally points in the opposite direction. However, they were more like Americans in gender and occupation (practice of law). Prospective citizen and professional legislators were fairly similar to each other in their social characteristics, although the well-educated, Republicans, and non-lawyers were more likely to be prospective citizen legislators. There were greater differences between retrospective citizen and professional legislators. The wealthier, the well-educated, and Republicans were more likely to be retrospective citizen legislators.

Geographical Constituency

The above analysis compares the pool of citizen legislators with that of professional legislators to see which group better reflects the American population. While this is one way to test whether citizen or professional legislators offer more descriptive representation, another way to test the proposition is to see whether citizen legislators are more similar to what Fenno (1977) termed the geographic constituency—people living in a member's district. That is, it is possible that citizen legislators better resemble their geographic constituency than professional legislators represent theirs. To estimate whether citizen legislators were more like their geographic constituency than were professional legislators to their constituency, we examined differences between members' characteristics and those of their districts. As with the above analysis we used politically relevant characteristics: race, education, income, gender, party, and age. However, we did not compare the percentage of members with law degrees to the districts since district level information was not available. To estimate members' characteristics, we used indicators that were based on the above analysis. Education was recoded such that members who had a college degree were coded one and others zero. This recoding was done so that the members' and districts' measures would be based on college education. Otherwise, the measures were coded the same as with the above analysis.

To estimate the characteristics of members' districts we used the *CQ's Congressional Districts of the 1990s* and *CQ's Politics in America 2002*.[10] To estimate race, we used the percentage of the district that was white. To estimate education, we used the percentage of the district that had a college degree. To estimate gender, we used the percentage of the district that was female. To estimate income we used the median income in thousands of dollars for each district standardized to 1999 dollars. Median age for the district was used to measure constituents' ages. The party make up of the district was calculated by averaging the percentage of the two-party vote that the member's party's presidential candidate received in 1992, 1996, and 2000.[11] For these measures the district's char-

Table 2.2. Demographic Differences Between Citizen and Professional Legislators: Geographic Constituency

	Prospective	Retrospective
Difference College	2.29+ (1.69)	-.12 (.74)
Difference Income	.0008+ (.0006)	.001* (.0005)
Difference Race	-2.85 (2.46)	-.61 (.87)
Difference Gender	9.56 (16.45)	-7.52 (6.42)
Difference Age	-.005 (.03)	.01 (.02)
Difference Party	7.35** (3.15)	1.78 (1.44)
Party (Democrat)	-.74 (.65)	-.41+ (.32)
103rd Congress	-.64 (.73)	.64+ (.42)
104th Congress	.14 (.67)	.82* (.43)
105th Congress	-.32 (.74)	.54 (.44)
Constant	-12.01+ (8.77)	-2.34 (3.43)
Cox and Snell R^2	.09	.08
Nagelkerke R^2	.19	.10
N	292	292
Chi^2	26.70**	23.04**

+< .20 * < .10 ** <.05 *** < .01 (using a two-tailed test)

Sources: *CQ's Biographies of Freshman Members* (various years), *CQ Politics in America*, http://www.Bioguide.congress.gov/biosearch/biosearch.asp, and *Financial Disclosure Reports of House Members* (various congresses). Data calculated by authors. See Appendix A for explanation of the variables.

acteristics were subtracted from the member's characteristics. For example, if the member was fifty years old and the median age of the district was thirty-five the difference would be fifteen. For race, if the member was white (coded one) and 78 percent of the district was white, the difference would be .22.

Since we were not interested in the direction of differences between members and their districts but just how similar they were to their districts, absolute numbers were used. The smaller the number, the more similar the member is to his or her district. The average difference for each of the variables was then calculated for prospective citizen and professional legislators, and retrospective citizen and professional legislators and then these differences were compared using OLS regression.

Findings

There was little evidence that members who were similar to their constituents were more likely to be citizen legislators, prospective and retrospective, than professional legislators (see Table 2.2). The less similar legislators were to their constituents with regard to education, income, and party, the more likely they were to be prospective citizen legislators.[12] Whereas the average member had a .04 chance of being a prospective citizen legislator, one that was one standard deviation above the mean in the college variable had a .06 probability and one that was one standard deviation above the mean in party difference had a .10 probability and one that was a standard deviation above the mean in the income difference had a .06 probability of being a prospective citizen legislator. These were the only significant relationships. Although there were some negative relationships, indicating closeness to their constituents, the only significant characteristic explaining being a retrospective citizen was income. While an average member had a .51 probability of being a retrospective citizen legislator, one that scored a standard deviation above the mean had a .58 probability. Whether Republicans were more likely to be retrospective citizen legislators neared statistical significance.

Conclusion

We find little evidence that citizen legislators, retrospective or prospective, were more similar to Americans or to their geographic constituents than were professional legislators. The findings were strong enough to conclude that citizen legislators did not offer more descriptive representation; however, they were not strong enough to conclude that they were a more elite group than were professional legislators, although the findings leaned in that direction.

Our findings beg the question: "Why were citizen legislators not like the citizens they represent?" The most plausible answer is that average Americans are unlikely to be elected given our current political system. Average Americans cannot raise the hundreds of thousands of dollars to run a campaign. Average Americans do not want to uproot their families and move to Washington, D.C. or face the media's scrutiny, nor can average Americans leave their jobs for a few years and then return to them. Many Americans have little interest in politics, making it unlikely that they would want to make gaining office their life's focus. Finally, the American voter does not want to elect a typical American but someone she perceives as better than typical Americans.

There was no support for the expectation that compared to professional legislators citizen legislators offered greater descriptive representation. If anything, there was a tendency for professional legislators as a group to be more reflective of the general population. If citizen legislators were likely to better represent the interests of their constituents because they have similar experiences to their constituents, these findings suggest citizen legislators should not differ from professional legislators in their ability to represent their constituents. If this were the only reason to argue that citizen legislators are preferred, we could stop here. However, other reasons have been offered as to why citizen legislator could be preferred. Members can know their districts' interests by keeping in contact with their constituents. In the next chapter, we examine whether citizen or professional legislators keep in better contact with their constituents.

Notes

1. These are two ways that assure some proportionality. However, it may be that different electoral systems such as single transferable vote or cumulative voting could increase proportionality.

2. Another reason citizen legislators might increase descriptive representation revolves around the incumbency advantage. Incumbent House members are highly likely to win reelection, making it difficult for institutional change to reflect changes in the population or in their attitudes. If incumbents were barred from seeking reelection, there would be more open seats and a greater probability of different types of people being elected. However, this argument does not suggest that citizen legislators per se will naturally be similar to the American people or that retrospective or prospective citizen legislators elected at one time will differ from others elected at the same time. Instead, it focuses on the effects that greater turnover will have on diversity

3. This statement of course ignores independents. If we assume independents lean evenly toward both parties, the make-up of Congress likely reflects the partisan make-up of America. Congress and the general public are fairly evenly split between Democrats and Republicans. However, Congress does not descriptively reflect the population that is apolitical or independent.

4. These data have their own set of problems. Since the income was for the year prior to entering Congress, their yearly incomes may be lower than normal since they were campaigning for office. Also, members do not report their spouses' incomes. Thus, some members list virtually no income but noted that their spouses were employed. Also, there were a few members whose financial disclosure forms were missing.

5. To standardize the scores, the inflation calculator supplied by the Bureau of Labor Statistics on its web page, http://bls.gov/cpi/home.htm, was used.

6. Information on members' race comes from http://www.house.gov/ebjohnson /cbcformermembers.htm and http://users.visi.net/~rmarin/hl_106?home.html. We did not break minority racial groups down into specific categories because the number of minority members was too small.

7. While it has been argued that the parties in the United States do not dramatically differ in ideology or issue positions, the 1990s were a period of heightened homogeneity and polarization of the parties (Aldrich and Rohde 2000, 2001).

8. When all the members who signed the pledge were treated as prospective citizen legislators, the education and law variables were no longer statistically significant. Appendix B, however, would suggest by eliminating those who exhibited progressive ambition, citizen legislators were less likely to practice law, more likely to be female, older, and wealthier.

9. The average member is one that scored at the mean on the variables, when the mean was for ordinal or nominal data, the score was rounded to the nearest whole number. Thus, the average here is more likely to a citizen legislator than the mean. We went a standard deviation below the mean, since the average member was at the highest score on education.

10. The data are based on the 1990 census. The district boundaries of a few members changed during the 1990s due to court cases involving majority minority districts. Because of this, data from *CQ's Politics in America 2002* was used for members who were elected from these districts and entered after 1996. *CQ's Congressional District* data were used for the old districts.

11. These data were taken from *CQ's Politics in America*. For members representing districts that were redrawn in the mid 1990s, only the 1996 and 2000 data were available.

12. When all the members who signed the pledge were treated as prospective citizen legislators, the difference college and the difference income variables were not significant. Appendix B indicates that the education variable had less effect on whether a member was a prospective citizen legislator, but gender and age had an increased effect.

Chapter Three
Constituency Relations

Good representatives understand the issues that affect their constituents. It is self-evident that a representative acting as a delegate must know the district's preferences, but trustees too must know the constituents' interests. It is on the basis of that knowledge that the trustee can weigh the alternatives and arrive at an optimal judgment and work on the constituents' behalf. Regardless of whether constituents' interests are determined through a delegate or trustee approach, members need to know how to deal with them. A reasonable way to learn about constituents is for there to be some contact between the member and his or her district.

That legislators and constituents need to be in contact with each other was noted by the Founders. The First Amendment of the Bill of Rights guarantees the right to petition the government. While constituent grievances may be characterized as complaints about government public policies, it can also extend to demanding specific government policies and actions. Constituents do let their members know of their needs and wishes by phone calls to the district office, e-mails, letters, personal visits, and through lobbyists for organized groups. Some of these contacts concern individuals' unique personal circumstances, while other contacts concern national or international policies.

Contacting constituents is important, because it gives members an opportunity to explain their Washington activities to their constituents. As Richard Fenno (1977) discusses, when members are visiting their districts, they need to be able to justify their activities, most notably their votes. How members explain their activities varies, but the main goal is to increase voters' trust and support of them. Another value of members discussing their votes is to inform and educate the public. Representation can be seen as a two-way street. Not only do constituents tell their representatives what they want, but policy makers also need to use their knowledge and expertise to educate their constituents.

One criticism leveled against professional representatives is their failure to maintain contact with their districts. When House member Richard Shelby (R-AL) was running against the incumbent, Sen. Jeremiah Denton (R-AL) in 1986, he used such a criticism. Showing a low-quality personal video of Sen. Denton telling an audience that he was too busy with national issues to pat baby bottoms in Alabama, Shelby successfully painted a picture of a disconnected representative more concerned about national issues than those state and local issues pertinent to Alabamians. At issue was a member focusing on matters important inside the Capitol at the expense of the concerns of the district's citizens. Whether this critique of long-serving politicians is correct is debatable. Below we discuss how ambition theory predicts that prospective citizen legislators have less contact with constituents than do professional legislators. Remember that prospective legislators are thought to have more discrete, i.e., less static and progressive, ambition. Thus, the desire for reelection will be missing and limit their need for contact with the district. However, theories about experience predict retrospective citizen legislators to have more contact. They may have more contact since they may need to learn more about the district beyond the immediate area that they came from.

Ambition theory predicts that prospective citizen legislators should have less contact with their constituents. This predicted relationship is because members' ambition affects constituency contact in so far that they work today to reach tomorrow's constituency (Schlesinger 1966). If keeping in contact with constituents enables members to gain or maintain their desired positions, members will keep in contact. In fact, research finds that members who want either reelection (static ambition) or election to a higher office (progressive ambition) will keep in greater contact with their constituents than those with discrete ambition (Herrick and Moore 1993). Thus, prospective citizen legislators should be less inclined to emphasize contacts with constituents.

Part of the reason that ambition affects the amount of contact members have with constituents is that members need to face reelection to keep their jobs. Prospective citizen legislators are assumed to be less reelection-focused than professional legislators, since they have more discrete ambition. Reelection concerns are thought to keep members accountable and responsive to the citizen. A classic example of the drive to satisfy constituents in order to stay in office is that of Lyndon Baines Johnson during his time as the personal secretary to Rep. Richard Kleberg (D-TX). It was in the midst of the Great Depression and many citizens, in and out of Texas, looked to the federal government for relief (Caro 1981, 214-60). LBJ saw constituency service as the foundation for political office. As Rep. Kleberg's assistant, he consciously made sure that everyone knew that he was responsible for Kleberg's actions in response to constituent requests. LBJ made sure that Kleberg's district received the federal government's financial benefits: "Whatever the New Deal program, Johnson reaped for his district every dollar it could provide" (Caro 1981, 259). By intently seeking contact with citizens and responding to their requests of the federal government, he was able to claim credit. This continued into his tenure as a representative and beyond.

Empirical evidence, too, provides some support for the idea that members with greater electoral needs will keep in greater contact with their constituents. Members who have announced they are leaving Congress and no longer face reelection take fewer trips home and allocate less staff to the district (Herrick, Moore, and Hibbing 1994). However, Fenno (1977) and Hibbing (1991) examined the number of trips members take back to their districts and the amount of staff in the district and found weak relationships between these two factors and vote percentage. This however does not rule out the possibility that that the drive for reelection still affects members' contact with constituents but that all members are equally driven for reelection. Jacobson (1987) argues that even with the incumbency advantage, members' still work hard serving their constituents so that they do not lose reelection. Despite the incumbency advantage, about one third of the membership eventually loses reelection, so it is no wonder that members work diligently not to be one of the fallen. Thus, it is likely that the desire to win reelection encourages members to keep in contact. Following from this, prospective citizen legislator, and possibly retrospective citizen legislators who may have less ambition, will be less reelection-focused and have few incentives to keep in contact with constituents.

While the lack of ambition for a long career is expected to limit prospective citizen legislators from keeping in contact, the lack of experience may increase retrospective citizen legislators' contact. Seniority or career stages are expected to affect constituent contact. Fenno (1977) finds that newer members are focused on building their coalitions and thus work hard to keep in touch and serve their districts, but the longer members stay in office, the less focused they are in expanding their coalitions and the more interested they are in maintaining them. He finds that newer members spend more time making trips and allocate more staff to the district than more senior members do. Since retrospective members are in an earlier career stage than members entering with some previous experience, we would expect them to be more focused on building coalitions and doing more to contact their constituents. However, prospective citizen legislators are closer to the end of their career so they should be less interested in building electoral coalitions and keeping contact with their constituents.

Fenno (1977) also found that personal reasons can affect members' contact with their districts. Members take more trips home if they are fairly inexpensive in time and money and if their families live in the district. Also, members will take fewer trips home if they have more staff in the district. Based on these findings we expect that citizen legislators, retrospective and prospective, will take more trips home, because they are likely to still have interests and needs in the district, but that the trips may be used to meet personal obligations not political ones.

Based on the above, differences between retrospective and prospective citizen legislators should be expected. Generally, it is expected that prospective citizen legislators will have less constituent contact than prospective professional legislators. In fact, research on term limits at the state level found that term-limited members (members who are similar to prospective citizen legislators in that they have a limited time in their current post) are less likely to keep in contact with their constituents than are non-term-limited members (Carey et al. 2000; Niemi and Powell 2003). Conversely, it is expected that retrospective citizen legislators will have greater contact with their constituents than professional legislators have with their constituents.

Measuring Members' Contact with their Districts

Although there are several ways to measure how members keep in contact with their district, we focus on three. First we examined the amount of money spent by members on trips to their districts. Returning to their home districts represents a very visible means of showing their concern and interest in the district and offers members a way to present themselves. While others (Fenno 1977; Hibbing 1991; Herrick and Moore 1993; Herrick, Moore, and Hibbing 1994) have examined the number of trips made by members, we used disbursements because in more recent congresses only disbursements for travel were recorded. This creates two weaknesses. One weakness is getting an accurate count on the number of trips members take back to their districts because of the vagaries of airline ticket pricing. Another weakness is that disbursements include staff travel as well as member travel. This may be an advantage, however, since member's staff going to the district also would indicate a desire on the part of members to keep in contact with their constituents. The more money spent is assumed to mean more frequent visits to the district and a heightened sensitivity to constituents.

The second measure that is utilized as an indicator of contact with the district is the percentage of staff members in district offices compared to the Washington office (Fenno 1977; Hibbing 1991; Herrick and Moore 1993; Herrick, Moore, and Hibbing 1994). Devoting more staff to the district enables representatives to maintain closer contact. Besides taking calls, staff members become an extension of the representative to the community in very visible ways. To measure the number of staff in the home and Washington offices, the *Congressional Directory* was used. It lists the names of staff in the member's Washington office and those in the home district where there may be multiple offices. While it is not unusual for the staff numbers to change over the legislative session, this is the best measure available. We collected data from the 103rd to 107th Congresses. Since members differ in how many staffers they have, we focus on the percentage of staffers members have in their districts instead of the number of staff in the district.

The third measure is the use of the franking privilege and is based on the amount of money spent on sending postal material (newsletters, constituent letters, etc.) from the Capitol Hill office. Although the district newsletter is often seen as a campaign tool, it also offers members a vehicle for educating their constituents, and it is a valuable method of credit-claiming and advertising (Mayhew 1974, 50). Highlighting federal grants to the district, pictures of meetings with important officials, such as the president if from the same party, and pictures with citizen groups from the district are some of the many items that appear. The point of the newsletter is to show constituents the representative's strong connection to the district, and to show concern for the district. Others, too, have examined newsletters as a method of understanding members' relationships with constituents (Canon 1999). We measured the amount of money spent on franking. Both the travel and frank information come from the Clerk of

Table 3.1. OLS Regression Equations Comparing Citizen Legislators with Professional Legislators in Contact with the District

	Travel	% Staff in District	Franking
Prospective	-3125.72	-.03	-378.79
	(3234.85)	(.04)	(4885.49)
Retrospective	883.65	.02	2232.46
	(1989.36)	(.02)	(3004.46)
Electoral Security	-6476.02	-.29*	-55707.53***
	(10169.60)	(.13)	(15358.82)
Intra-institutional	1411.01	.07*	-483.16
	(3148.80)	(.04)	(4755.54)
Progressive Ambition	4635.91*	-.06*	-4715.16
	(2699.18)	(.03)	(4076.48)
District Age	-583.99+	-.00	512.20
	(383.82)	(.01)	(579.66)
District Education	-31372.23**	.31**	81232.01***
	(12508.18)	(.15)	(18890.72)
103th Congress	-6833.84**	-.05+	-953.93
	(2751.83)	(.04)	(4156.00)
104th Congress	-11195.79***	.07*	-516.49
	(2931.65)	(.04)	(4427.58)
105th Congress	-1797.14	.04	-5367.05
	(2894.79)	(.04)	(4371.91)
Virginia/Maryland	-22204.25***	-.01	-8804.55
	(5413.80)	(.07)	(8176.29)
Party	-4795.25**	.01	9067.07***
	(2226.69)	(.03)	(3362.89)
Constant	66659.03***	.35*	39731.55*
	(14666.84)	(.19)	(22150.87)
R^2	.19	.12	.16
Adj. R^2	.15	.08	.12
N	252	271	252

+< .20 * < .10 ** <.05 *** < .01 (using a two-tailed test)
Data sources: *Congressional Directory*, *CQ's Biographies of Freshman Members* (various years), *CQ's Congressional Districts of the 1990s*, *CQ's Politics in America 2002*, travel and franking forms kept with the Clerk of the House. Data calculated by authors. See Appendix A for explanation of variables.

the House. The forms for some of the members were missing, primarily those who did not serve a third term. Consequently, there were fewer cases for these analyses.

To estimate whether citizen or professional legislators should keep in better contact with their constituents, we use OLS regression to control for several factors. In addition to the controls described in Chapter One, we control for type of ambition, reelection prospects, and proximity of the district to Washington, D.C. Progressive ambition was measured by whether a member exhibited progressive ambition (coded one if the member sought a higher office, otherwise, coded zero). Second, we measured intra-institutional ambition by whether a member sought a leadership position in the House (coded one if the member sought a leadership position; otherwise coded zero). Members were coded as having either progressive or intra-institutional ambition even if they sought a higher position after their first two congresses. Ambition was defined as desire to obtain a position rather than actually having the position.

We also controlled for reelection prospects. We controlled for variation in members' electoral security by measuring the strength of their party in their districts. Electoral security was measured as mean percentage of the district's vote going to the presidential candidate of the representative's party in 1992, 1996, and 2000.[1] We examined party strength instead of vote received in members' reelection efforts since members may not know if they face a quality challenger and the competitive nature of their re-election bid until late in a term. As such, it would not affect their behaviors early in a term. However, they were likely to know if they represent a district likely to swing to the other party. Although reelection needs have usually been found to have little effect on a representative's attention to the district, we controlled for differences in members' reelection prospects since they are commonly thought to affect members' contact with their constituents. Fifth, we controlled for variations in district characteristics. Some districts expect more attention from their members than others (Fenno 1977). Since we lacked a direct measure of district preferences, we controlled for levels of education, and median age in the districts. We expected that districts with less educated, and older constituents to want more contact from their member. Finally, we controlled for proximity of members' districts to Washington, D.C. with a dummy variable coded one if the member represents Virginia or Maryland, otherwise zero.

Findings

The findings offer weak support for the idea that prospective citizen legislators are less likely to keep in contact with their constituents than are prospective professional legislators, and that retrospective citizen legislators keep in more contact with their constituents than retrospective professional legislators. On all three measures of citizen contact prospective citizen legislators scored lower than others but the differences were quite small.[2] They spent about $3100 less on travel, had 3 percent fewer staffers in the district and spent about $378 less on the frank. But none of the differences were statistically significant. On the other hand, retrospective citizen legislators tended to keep in more contact. They spent about $884 more on travel, had about 2 percent more staff in the district, and spent about $2232 more on the frank. Again, none of these differences even approached normal levels of statistical significance. The models used to predict citizen contact did a moderate job in predicting who contacted their constituents. The Adj. R^2s ranged from .08-15, and district education, party, electoral security, and progressive ambition explain most of the difference.

Presumably the reason prospective citizen legislators were less likely to keep in contact was because they were less interested in reelection. Rep. Tom Allen (D-ME), a professional legislator, thought that members from marginal districts have the least freedom to ignore constituent wishes: "That's the great divide here, the great divide between people who can more or less do what they think is right and those that are always looking over their shoulder" (2004). But he also feels, based on his experience, all members care about their constituents.

Although there was little difference between citizen and professional legislators with regard to travel, the importance of this variable may be suspect as citizen legislators may return home for personal reasons. For example, former Rep. Mark Sanford (R-SC), a prospective citizen legislator, decided not to move his family to Washington. In his book (2000) he writes he "would sleep on a futon in my office and shower at the House gym. Even today when I go back to South Carolina, one of the things people often ask is whether or not I am still sleeping in my office: to them, it is a sign I haven't gone native" (14). Tom Coburn (R-OK), as will be discussed in Chapter Six, continued his medical practice while in office, delivering babies on the weekends in his district. As a doctor planning to return to his practice full time when he left Congress, he needed to maintain the practice and his skills. While delivering babies is honorable, it is not likely to give a member the same understanding of the district as other kinds of constituent contact.

Professional politicians, in contrast, use their time in the district to speak to voters. Our interview with Rep. Frank Lucas (R-OK), a professional legislator, indicates the importance he saw in maintaining contact with the district, and more importantly, in explaining his actions in Congress when he was in the district. He views this contact as a two-way street. He learns his constituents' priorities and he educates his constituents about his votes: "I use my town meetings, my newsletter, my weekly column, my radio shows, to try and educate my constituents and bring them along with me to a level of understanding so that when I cast a vote on their behalf I try to have a consensus that I work from" (Lucas 2004).

Conclusions

How much contact members have with their home districts is important to understanding their representational style. Maintaining contact with constituents is often expected to be more important for professional legislators than for citizen legislators since that contact is key to successful reelection, although other theories suggest that citizen legislators may have other reasons to stay in contact with their districts. The findings in this chapter show that the differences between citizen and professional legislators were slight, but that prospective citizen legislators had slightly less contact with their districts than others and retrospective citizen legislators had more contact.

Although there were few significant differences between our citizen and professional legislators, one factor that had strong effects on the amount of staff in the district and use of the frank was electoral security. Members who represented marginal districts did more to stay in contact with others, indicating that elections, at least competitive elections, serve to make members more responsive. The interviews also suggested that members' reelection needs affected how much contact they have with their constituents.

The effects of progressive ambition also shed some light on the role of ambition and elections. The findings suggest that members with progressive ambition make more trips home and have less staff in the district. Those with progressive ambition may keep staff in D.C. to work on policy interests of concern to the larger constituency. And the trips back home may be used not only to keep their constituents happy but they could easily travel to surrounding areas where future constituents could reside.

One of the reasons to examine descriptive representation in the previous chapter and members' contact with the district in this chapter was to examine ways members may get to know the interests of their constituents. Although we find in these two chapters little evidence that citizen legislators should have greater knowledge of their constituents' interests because of similarity to their constituents or greater contact with them, they could still offer greater substantive representation. This could occur either because they represent more homogeneous districts, which are easier to know or because voters who choose citizen legislators are somehow more likely to select people who know their interests. In the next chapter we examine whether citizen or professional legislators are likely to offer greater substantive representation.

Notes

1. Because of court ordered redistricting in the middle of the decade, the scores for some members leave out the 1992 election and, in some cases, the 1996 election.

2. When all members who signed the pledge were considered to be prospective citizen legislators, the coefficients were larger (more negative) but still not statistically significant. Appendix B indicates that there would be little difference in the findings had we excluded from the list of prospective citizen legislators those who exhibited progressive ambition.

Chapter Four
Substantive Representation

A common way to think of representation is what Pitkin (1967) called substantive or "acting for" representation; that representatives work for their constituents. What voters want is their representative to act in their interest. In this chapter, we explore whether citizen or professional legislators are more inclined to vote consistently with their constituents' wishes.

Since the creation of the United States, it has been argued that professional politicians would become a ruling class isolated from their constituents' everyday trials and tribulations. Gilbert Livingston, a delegate to New York's ratifying convention, said:

> In such a situation, [long service], men are apt to forget their dependence, lose their sympathy, and contract selfish habits. Factions are apt to be formed, if the body becomes permanent. The senators will associate only with men of their own class, and thus become strangers to the conditions of the common people. They should not only return, and be obliged to live with the people, but return to their former rank of citizenship, both to revive their sense of dependence, and to gain knowledge of the country (qtd. in Malbin 1992, 57).

The substantial amount of research on whether members who are predominately professional legislators understand and make decisions consistent with the wishes of their constituents has had mixed findings. A few examples illustrate the point. On one hand, some research finds members' roll-call votes to be influenced by their constituents' preferences. Kingdon's model of congressional voting (1989), for example, indicates that members will vote the wishes of their voters if the voters have a preference. Holian, Krebs, and Walsh (1997) found that members voted the wishes of their constituents on NAFTA. On the other hand, other research, such as the Miller and Stokes (1963), found more modest relationships between constituent preferences and roll-call votes, depending on the saliency of the issue to constituents, and the homogeneity of constituents' preferences. Similarly, Bernstein (1989) found little congruence between constituent preferences and members' roll-call votes, most voters were not knowledgeable as to members' votes (Bernstein 1989, 99). Additionally, he found that the longer the member stays in Congress, the smaller is the congruence between members and constituents (Bernstein 1989, 102).

Not only has the research on constituent preferences and members' roll-call votes been mixed, so too has the research on members' understanding of constituents' preferences. For example, while Miller and Stokes found modest relationships dependent on policy area, Herrera, Herrera, and Smith (1992) found that although members' positions were more extreme than their constituents' positions, they were fairly close, and members could position themselves near their constituents' preferences. They too found some variation by policy area. Thus, although arguments that members are out of touch with their constituents are exaggerated, members could be more reflective of their constituents' preferences. However, that does not necessarily imply that citizen legislators will be more representative, and we are skeptical that they would be.

One way that citizen legislators are thought to be better substantive representatives is that they are more motivated to serve the public's interest than are professional legislators because they have weaker political ambitions. Research on term-limited members (who are similar to prospective citizen legislators) at the state level finds that term-limited members serve out of policy goals not career goals (Herrick and Thomas 2005). Similarly, Costantini and Valenty (1996) find that activists without "ambition" have more extreme ideological rigidity than those with purposive motivations.[1] Even if citizen legislators are more policy motivated than are professional legislators, it may not mean that the members will be working for the preferences of the district. If their policy goals or interests overlap with their constituents' interests, they could be more representative. However, if they do not match, then they would be less representative, working on and supporting issues that are not in the interest of their constituents. Also, if the district is not homogeneous in its support of the member's position, the member may be more likely to work counter to even significant minority interests. This would be a particularly troubling sign as democracy depends on the inclusion of minority views for the legitimacy of the process. Ideologues representing districts with constituents like themselves may be less likely to hear minority voices.

Ambition too may affect members' responsiveness to constituents' interests by altering their concern about reelection. Ambition for a future career in politics is dependent on reelection, and reelection is designed to keep members responsive to voters. As Schlesinger points out, "[r]epresentative government, above all, depends on a supply of men so driven; the desire for election and, more important, for reelection becomes the electorate's restraint upon its public officials. No more irresponsible government is imaginable than one of high minded men unconcerned for their political futures" (1966, 2). Much congressional research supports this idea. First, research that examines members' behavior after they announce they are not seeking reelection finds that they change their behaviors. Members alter their ideological voting patterns in their last congress (Zupan 1990; Carey 1994; Rothenberg and Sanders 2000). Second, research finds that electoral concerns increase constituent preference and roll-call congruence. Kuklinski (1978) examined the roll-call behavior in California's legislature and found that the frequency of elections increased the likelihood that legislators voted their constituents' preferences. Electoral vulnerability too has been found to affect constituent preference and roll-call congruence. Holian,

Krebs, and Walsh (1997) found that electorally vulnerable members were more likely to vote their constituents' preferences on the North American Free Trade Act (NAFTA). Similarly, members' votes on GATT (General Agreement on Trade and Tariffs) were influenced by constituents' interests and members' vulnerability (Gartzke and Wrighton 1998). Hibbing's (1984) examination of "transfer payment voting"[2] found that the smaller the members' previous vote percentage the more likely they were to support transfer payments while those not seeking reelection were less likely to. Similarly, he found that the more proximate Republican senators' reelection, the more likely they were to support such policies.

There are some potential limitations of electoral constraints. First, the incumbency advantage means few members are electorally vulnerable. That most members are virtually assured reelection means that they can ignore constituents without fear of losing their seat. While this seems logical, Jacobson (1987), as noted earlier, finds the contrary; members run scared and work hard to reach their constituents. A second problem is that most voters are not attentive enough to punish members who work on issues not in their wishes. Bernstein (1989) found that in most cases, constituents did not control their representatives. "Members who have 'gone astray' are rarely replaced, and if they are replaced because they have gone astray, it is unlikely that the 'common citizen' is doing the replacing. Elections do not serve as a 'mechanism through which citizens control their government'" (Bernstein 1989, 98). Attentive citizens seek to reward and punish representatives based on their issue positions; however, their numbers are so small that incumbents are still likely to win (Bernstein 1989, 99). However, this does not mean that citizen legislators would be better representatives, but just that there would be little or no difference between them and professional legislators. These limitations aside, we believe that elections increase the congruence between members' behavior and constituents' preferences, and that citizen legislators have less incentive to get to know and work on their constituents' interests. Both prospective and retrospective citizen legislators are thought to be less interested in reelection; prospective, because they know they have a limited time to serve, and retrospective, because they are more likely to have a job to return to back home.

A reason citizen legislators are thought to be better representatives of their constituents is that they have experiences of private citizens not of politicians. However, the evidence from Chapter Two points to holes in this argument. Although citizen legislators may not be a "ruling class" they do not share the socio-demographic characteristics of their constituents. Like the professional legislators, we study citizen legislators were wealthier and better educated than most Americans. Consequently, they are not likely to share the real life experiences of their working and middle class constituents.

Not only does the above discussion offer little reason to expect citizen legislators to be better representatives than professional legislators, but, also, there are reasons to expect political experience to increase legislators' ability to offer substantive representation. First, if members want to cast votes based on their constituents' preferences, they have to know their preferences. We expect that citizen legislators, particularly retrospective citizen legislators, will have less knowledge of the district, since they lack experience serving the district's constituents. This view is consistent with statements made by Madison in *Federalist #56* when he assumed members would know their district by having served it. This is even more likely today as an average House district has over 650,000 residents. An average citizen is unlikely to have direct experiences with a very representative sample of the entire district.

Based on the above, we do not expect citizen legislators to be better substantive representatives than professional legislators. They will be more ideologically extreme and less likely to support the districts' preferences. To test these expectations we examine roll-call behaviors in two areas: ideology and party support.

Are Citizen Legislators More Ideologically Extreme than Professional Legislators?

If citizen legislators are motivated for policy reasons and are unconstrained by reelection or unfamiliar with their constituents and legislative processes, it is likely that they will be more ideologically extreme. To test whether citizen or professional legislators are more extreme we used two measures.

First, to estimate members' ideology we examined their DW-NOMINATE dimension 1 scores. These scores are based on roll-call votes and range from -1 to 1. The more positive a member's score the more conservative a member is considered to be.[3] Because we were not interested in the direction of ideology but in the strength of a representative's ideology, we used absolute scores. We averaged each member's DW-NOMINATE scores over his or her first two congresses.

We examined roll-call votes knowing full well the weaknesses of such data: roll-call votes do not reflect the intensity of the action; they occur late in the process so may be less important than committee work; they assume nonstrategic voting by members; and they are not fully comparable across congresses. However, we believed there is value to examining roll-call votes. Research on roll-call voting indicates that such behavior is predictable in a meaningful sense. Second, it was possible. While it is also possible to examine bills introduced and committee work focusing on a particular issue, it is less feasible to look at all bills a member introduced and determine if they helped each district specifically. We also believed that the case studies helped fill the gap created by examining roll-call votes.

To determine whether citizen or professional legislators were more ideological in their voting, we used Ordinary Least Squares (OLS) regression to control for several factors that could cause spurious relationships. In addition to the usual controls we controlled for members' electoral security. We expect elections to constrain members' behavior. Thus, we would expect that members who served electorally secure districts were freer to vote their own preferences instead of those of their constituents. To measure electoral security we use our measure of party strength in the district. We do this for the reasons discussed in Chapter Three.

If citizen legislators were ideologues, we would expect them to have higher party support/unity scores than if they were less ideological in their voting. Although it could be that ideologues would be unwilling to sacrifice their principles to toe the party line during the time period we examined, ideologues were more likely to support the party since congressional parties were more extreme and polarized (Bond and Fleisher 2000). To measure party unity we calculated members' average party unity scores (corrected for non-attendance) for their first two congresses as provided in *CQ Weekly Reports* (various years). We use the same controls as noted above plus members' ideology measured as the true DW-NOMINATE scores—not the absolute.

Findings: Ideology, Partisanship, and Citizen Legislators

When measuring ideology using DW-NOMINATE scores, there was strong evidence that citizen legislators, prospective and retrospective, were more ideologically extreme. Both types of citizen legislators had statistically significantly more extreme positions than others (Table 4.1, Column A).[4] The strength of members' ideology was also affected by members' party, electoral security, and when they entered the House. Republicans and members coming from safe districts were much more ideological. Generally, the relationships between these characteristics and strength of ideology were in the predicted direction and the model explained about 35 percent of the variance in members' absolute DW-NOMINATE scores.

When partisan voting was used as an indication of ideological voting, the findings were significantly different (Table 4.2, Column A). Prospective citizen legislators were less ideological and retrospective citizen legislators were similar to professional legislators. The other factors in the models, particularly those related to political parties, had strong relationship with party support. The model was able to explain over 60 percent of the variance in party support (Adjusted $R^2=.62$). The reason for the divergent findings is that the citizen legislators were so ideologically extreme that they would not compromise their principles for their party. Rep. Tom Coburn (R-OK) and other retrospective and prospective citizen legislators such as Rep. Steve Largent (R-OK) participated in a revolt against the party leadership for bargaining too much with the Democrats. Moreover, Coburn describes in his book (2003) his critique of his party for not being principled enough. Based on these observations we tend to believe that the DW-NOMINATE scores offer a better picture of ideological voting. Thus, we believe that citizen legislators were more ideologically extreme.

Table 4.1. OLS Regression Equations Comparing Citizen and Professional Legislators' Ideological Scores

Variable	A	B	C
Prospective	.05**	-.15	.05+
	(.03)	(.25)	(.03)
Retrospective	.04**	.01	.14+
	(.02)	(.02)	(.09)
Party	-.11***	-.66***	-.65***
	(.02)	(.02)	(.02)
Electoral Security	.85***	-.13	-.14+
	(.08)	(.10)	(.10)
103rd Congress	-.04*	-.02	-.02
	(.02)	(.03)	(.03)
104th Congress	-.00	.06**	.06*
	(.03)	(.03)	(.03)
105th Congress	-.03+	.03	.03
	(.03)	(.03)	(.03)
District Republican	—	.85***	.78***
		(.10)	(.11)
Pro * District Rep.	—	.38	—
		(.47)	
Retro * District Rep.	—	—	.031*
			(.17)
Constant	-.01	.02	.05
	(.05)	(.09)	(.10)
R^2	.37	.91	.91
Adj. R^2	.35	.90	.90
N	257	257	257

+< .20 * < .10 ** <.05 *** < .01 (using a two-tailed test)

Sources: *Almanac of American Politics* (various years), http://www.voteview.com/dwnomin.htm, *CQ*'s *Biographies of Freshman Members* (various years), *CQ*'s *Politics in America 2002*. Data calculated by authors. See Appendix A for an explanation of the variables.

The dependent variable for column A is the absolute DW-NOMINATE score.

Column A tests whether prospective citizen or professional legislator and whether retrospective citizen or professional legislators were more likely to have ideological votes.

Column B tests whether prospective citizen or professional legislators were more likely to vote the ideological preferences of their constituents.

Column C tests whether retrospective citizen or professional were more likely to vote the ideological preferences of their constituents.

Is There Greater Congruence Between Citizen Legislators' Behavior and their Constituents' Ideology than Between Professional Legislators' Behavior and their Constituents' Ideology?

One of the key points of substantive representation is that members work in the interests of their constituents. To examine whether citizen or professional legislators were more supportive of their constituents' interests we used two measures that focus on members' preferences and constituents' preferences. Generally, we examined whether one acts more like a delegate than the other. First, we wanted to know if members voted in accord with the ideological leanings of the districts. To determine the ideological leanings of the district we used the districts' vote for president. We assumed that districts more likely to support Democratic presidential candidates were more liberal than those supporting Republicans. Here we calculated the percentage of the district's two-party vote going to the Republican presidential candidate in each member's district in 1992, 1996, and 2000.[5] This is at best an imprecise indicator of district leanings, but polling data by congressional district are collected infrequently, and using party vote as an indicator of constituents' preferences is not without precedent (Wright 2004). We then compared this score with the DW-NOMINATE scores for the members. Since we wanted to indicate how conservative a members' roll-call voting was, we did not use the absolute scores.

To determine if citizen legislators were more likely to act in the interests of their constituents we used OLS regression to control for the same factors used in the analysis of ideological voting. The key with the regression models is an interaction variable between whether a member was a citizen legislator and how Republican the district voted.

Another way that members could act in the interests of their constituents is to vote the party preferences of the voters. This assumes voters select parties based on the parties' platforms and once in office the parties work on their platforms. Although the United States is usually not thought of as having a responsible party system, voters are still likely to vote for parties based on some view of what the party would do in office. We conducted a second analysis that parrallels that of examining whether citizen or professional legislators were more likely to vote the ideological preferences of the voters. The difference was that the dependent variable was party unity scores not DW-NOMINATE scores, and the key independent variables are not based on Republican presidential vote but vote for the presidential candidates of the member's party. In these analyses the key independent variable is the interaction variable of citizen legislator (prospective or retrospective) and party strength in the district.

Findings: Congruence and Citizen Legislators

The findings suggest that prospective citizen legislators do not differ from others in the degree to which they vote with the wishes of their districts: behave as

Table 4.2. OLS Regression Equations Comparing Citizen and Professional Legislators' Party Unity Scores

Variable	A	B	C
Prospective	-3.16*** (1.11)	-10.97 (10.44)	-3.15*** (1.11)
Retrospective	.61 (.71)	.57 (.71)	2.92 (4.57)
Party	-4.22*** (.83)	-4.16*** (.83)	-4.19*** (.83)
Absolute DW	36.62*** (2.78)	36.62*** (2.78)	36.68*** (2.78)
Party Strength	18.13*** (4.31)	17.54*** (4.38)	18.97*** (4.61)
103rd Congress	.27 (1.03)	.20 (1.03)	.31 (1.03)
104th Congress	-.45 (1.11)	-.50 (1.11)	-.44 (1.11)
105th Congress	-.36 (1.09)	-.40 (1.09)	-.33 (1.09)
Pro * Party Strength	—	14.31 (19.05)	—
Retro * Party Strength	—	—	4.11 (8.02)
Constant	65.45*** (2.14)	65.25*** (2.27)	64.91*** (2.39)
R^2	.63	.62	.63
Adj. R^2	.62	.61	.62
N	257	257	257

+< .20 * < .10 ** <.05 *** < .01 (using a two-tailed test)
Sources: *Almanac of American Politics* (various years), http://voteview.Com/dwnomin.htm, *CQ's Biographies of Freshman Members* (various years), *CQ's Politics in America 2002*. Data calculated by authors. See Appendix A for explanation of the variables.
Column A tests whether prospective citizen or professional legislators and whether retrospective citizen or professional legislators were more likely to have high party unity scores.
Column B tests whether prospective citizen or professional legislators were more likely to vote the party preferences of their constituents.
Column C tests whether retrospective citizen or professional legislators were more likely to vote the party preferences of their constituents.

delegates (Table 4.1 Column B). The interaction variable, being a prospective citizen legislator and Republican vote of the district, was positively related to ideological voting but was not statistically significant. Table 4.2 (Column B) indicates too that prospective citizen legislators do not differ significantly from professional legislator in whether they vote the party wishes of the district.[6] That is, the interaction variable between prospective citizen legislators and party preferences of the district was not statistically significant. The models explained about 90 percent of the variance in members' party unity scores and DW-NOMINATE scores. Two other factors explain most of the variance in members' party voting: DW-NOMINATE scores, party affiliation, and how the district votes. Also, two factors explain most of the variance in DW-NOMINATE scores: party and Republican strength in the district.

There is greater evidence that retrospective citizen legislators were more likely to vote the wishes of their constituents. In both equations the interaction variables between retrospective citizen legislators and constituents' wishes was positive with the relationship between the interaction variable and DW-NOMINATE variables being statistically significant. This finding offers some support for the view that citizen legislators who come from the private sphere will do a better job representing the interests of their constituents. Coupled with the findings from previous chapters, a picture emerges of retrospective citizen legislators that offers some support for the idea that those with less experience do more to find out their constituents' wishes and acts upon those wishes. However, this tendency is not pronounced.

A likely reason that the differences were not stronger is because of the importance members of all types place on representing their constituents. One congressional observer emphatically stated, "It's called the House of Representatives for a reason. If you come from Wisconsin and you say 'No, I don't care about dairy' you don't deserve to be serving in Congress because you are not there as a representative" (anon. 2004). With rare exceptions members follow this dictate to represent the specific local interests. This was evident in their committee assignments. Rep. Frank Lucas (R-OK), a professional legislator, even petitioned to serve on an extra committee (the Science Committee) in order to increase spending in his district. However, his primary concern is agriculture. "I spend lots of time on agriculture because that's the one issue that has the greatest impact on the broadest group of my constituents and they're the most keyed and focused" (Lucas 2004). Former Rep. Tillie Fowler (R-FL), who signed the term limits pledge, made sure she was on the Armed Services Committee to represent the military bases in her district. She was not able to prevent the closing of a major naval air station when she first assumed her seat, but she worked actively to preserve the remaining military installations that were important to the district's local economy. Former Rep. Bob Riley (R-AL) was in a similar situation. Even though he was term-limited, he still worked diligently to preserve local military installations from closure by Base Realignment and Closure (BRAC). Rep. Sue Kelly (R-NY), who had not previously held an elective office but had been a legislative aide, served on the Transportation and Infrastructure Committee, notorious for bringing home the pork. Maine has a great concern about the environmental impact of power plant emissions and its member Rep. Tom Allen (D-ME) served on the House Energy and Air Quality Subcommittee, which has responsibility for oversight on the EPA's enforcement of air quality standards.

Former Rep. Tillie Fowler (R-FL), also noted that she based political decisions on what she thought was right, not her constituents' preferences—behaving as a trustee. She got her philosophy for making and explaining political decisions from her father, a former Democratic politician from Georgia: "Decide what you think is the right thing to do and do it. Then let your constituents know what you did and why. And that was great advice because I found over through years that my constituents came to respect my process even when they didn't agree with my decision" (Fowler 2004). This demonstrates how representation is a two-way street. When Fowler voted against the wishes of the district, she educated the public as to why she thought her vote was right.

There were exceptions to the argument that citizens need to represent their constituents on the part of two citizen legislators. In his book, former Rep. Tom Coburn (2003), who was inexperienced and signed the term limits pledge, discusses the job of a representative, not in terms of being a representative of constituents but of principle. For example, while he rarely discusses members' responsibilities to their voters, he states the most important loyalty of members should be to the Constitution (2003, 19). He also believes that the sign of a mature politician is one who works on principle, "true maturity . . . is a persistent ability to stand on principle and pursue the long-term best interest of the country, not just their district or state, in the face of political danger" (Coburn 2003, 65). In 1998, the Transportation and Infrastructure Committee asked House members to review the highway dollars going to their districts. Coburn, along with a few other members, objected to the practice, seeing it as a way to force members to support the bill. Coburn ended up voting to reject $15 million dollars in spending for his district (Ota 1998; Coburn 2003). Another example comes from 1999 when Coburn led a filibuster by amendments on the agriculture appropriations bill to cut funding. One of the programs he tried to cut included $300,000 for peanut farmers, money that could have helped Oklahoma peanut farmers (Church 1999). Similarly, former Rep. Mark Sanford (R-SC) felt that term limits allowed him to focus on what he considered the larger issues and to cast votes, such as opposing the 1998 transportation bill (Sanford 2000, 75).

Although we did not find differences between prospective and professional legislators, our research does point to the importance of elections. Members' electoral security has an impact on their votes: the more secure, the more ideological the vote. The importance of elections is also supported by comments from a professional legislator. Rep. Allen (D-ME) believes members have room to vote in ways that constituents may not approve; however, this freedom is circumscribed by the margin of victory in the previous election. Rep. Allen notes that "For those who win by 50.5, 51, 52 percent of the vote year after year after year are more often voting in ways they don't quite believe in but they've got to protect themselves" (Allen 2004). For himself, Allen believes that a single vote will not make or break an election "so I can do what I think is right even if many of my constituents would find it hard to understand. But the truth is I still care what they think. I don't want to alienate people unnecessarily" (Allen 2004).

Conclusions

Substantive representation requires legislators to behave in a way that advances the interests of their constituents and not merely mirrors their constituents' characteristics. The findings here suggest that citizen legislators were more ideological than others in their voting. It also indicates that although prospective citizen legislators did not differ from others in the degree to which they voted the wishes of their constituents, retrospective citizen legislators were more likely to follow the districts' wishes.

To conclude, there were real but not dramatic differences between citizen and professional legislators with regard to substantive representation. While there were some significant findings, most were not. Much like our conclusions from the previous chapters we do not believe there were significant differences because "true" citizen legislators, those who are similar to the people and have little political savvy, are not likely to be elected. People who are not political are not likely to seek higher office, and even if they were, Americans are unlikely to vote for such candidates. Although members may be citizen legislators, in terms of motivations and expectations about length of service, they are not apolitical or typical of Americans. Other factors too increase the congruence between members and constituents, such as voters preferring candidates similar to themselves and the homogeneity of the district.

This chapter examined whether members voted according to the preferences of their district. This is but one way members work in the interests of constituents. In the next chapter we examine whether citizen or professional legislators are more active and effective in the legislative process.

Notes

1. Ambition, according to Constantini and Valenty (1996), is a motive for wanting a political career. Purposive motivations are held by politicians motivated to serve out of a desire to affect policy.

2. These are votes that increase payments to particular groups of people in the electorate.

3. The DW-NOMINATE data comes from http://voteview.com/dwnomin.htm. This website explains how the scores were calculated. We thank Poole and Rosenthal for making their data easily accessible.

4. When all members who signed the pledge were considered to be prospective citizen legislators, citizen legislators were not more ideologically extreme using the DW-

NOMINATE Scores. Appendix B indicates that the findings would be similar if the measure of citizen legislators excluded those exhibiting progressive ambition.

5. This is essentially the same measure as party strength but based on Republican support, not the members' party. This variable is highly correlated to the electoral security variable (r=.54; p=.00); however, since both variables were statistically significant in the equation, we left them both in.

6. When all members who signed the pledge were considered to be prospective citizen legislators the results were essentially the same. Again, Appendix B indicates that the findings would be similar had members exhibiting progressive ambition were excluded from the citizen legislators category.

Chapter Five
Effectiveness

Good representatives are effective legislators. Members who are not engaged and effective in policy making are not "acting for" their constituents. Identifying which members are effective is difficult because effectiveness is an illusive term. One way to think of an effective legislator is as "one who is able to incorporate her preferences, however they are induced, into a whole array of policy outputs" (Jeydel and Taylor 2003, 20). A common way to conceptualize such effectiveness is introducing legislation and seeing it become law (Frantzich 1979, 411; Olson and Nonidez 1972, 271). However, it can also include blocking legislation, affecting debates through the use of the media, serving on key committees, or simply showing up and casting roll-call votes. Although some may argue that citizen legislators will be more effective because they are assumed to be more focused on legislating instead of on career advancement, we believe they will be less effective. Citizen legislators likely have good intentions, will work hard, and be active participants in the legislation process. However, it is unlikely that they have the experience, skills, knowledge, and favors needed to build coalitions to support or oppose legislation. Lacking a desire for a long career too may limit their effectiveness by decreasing other members' willingness to mentor or bargain with them.

In 1979, Frantzich identified four theories that help explain legislative effectiveness.[1] One of these was experience theory, which predicts legislative experience increases members' effort and effectiveness since experience increases members' understanding of the process, issues, and power. As a point of illustration, Rep. Anthony Beilenson (D-CA) said the six-year limit on the House Permanent Select Committee on Intelligence resulted in many members of the committee not understanding the issues until their final two years on the committee.

> Even though virtually every member of the committee had had several years of experience in Congress, we had no one on the committee who had any experience overseeing the operations of the intelligence community that extended beyond six years. Most of us found that it took us about three or four years just to learn the intricacies of the issues involved in intelligence operations, and then we had just two years to really use that expertise—to be in a position where we could pose challenging questions to the heads of the CIA and other intelligence agencies and make sensible decision. (*Congressional Record* 1995, H3832)

The idea that experience or seniority is needed for members to be effective is demonstrated in the research by Frantzich (1979) and Hibbing (1991). They find that seniority increases members' ability to see the legislation they introduce pass.

One way to think of experience is the political experience possessed by members when they first arrive on Capitol Hill—retrospective experience. Common sense indicates that members arriving on Capitol Hill with previous political experience will be better able to hit the ground running and thus have more opportunities to achieve legislative and representative goals than will members lacking experience. Members with state legislative experience believe their experience gives them a better understanding of the issues, personalities, and processes of legislatures and an opportunity to learn from mistakes (Louison 1988; Boulard 1994). Berkman's research supports these impressions. Berkman (1993) argued that members with previous legislative experience had greater institutional mastery, "a broad understanding, aptitude, and appreciation for legislative life, norms, and politics, along with the skills to be an effective legislator" (80), and policy mastery, "expertise in a distinct policy area, along with knowledge of the interests and policy networks involved in policy debate and formulation" (81). Members who have legislative experience, particularly from professional legislatures, are better able to be effective early in their House career and to gain seats on prestige and policy committees. Professional legislatures typically have more resources for legislators, such as staff and legislative research support. Members with little prior experience are less likely than legislators with prior political experience to become leaders (Boulard 1994; Louison 1988). Members need political knowledge and skills to win the respect of their colleagues and to be voted in as leaders, and those coming to office without previously having held a political office lack that experience.

Although members without previous experience are likely less effective, they may not necessarily be less active. Little and Moore (1996), for example, found that members with previous legislative experience were less likely to be active.[2] Similarly, Frantzich (1979) found members with previous political experience sponsored significantly fewer bills than others. However, both works were examining the apprenticeship norm, which required freshmen members to be less active. They argued that members with previous experience would know the norms and be less active. However, in the time period we examined, the apprenticeship norm was no longer in effect. Thus, there is less reason to expect members with experience to limit their activities.

Although the experience theory as expressed is unlikely to affect prospective citizen legislators, the fact that they will not have future experiences limits their ability to become effective policy makers. Prospective citizen legislators are limited in their ability to make long-term deals or deals involving a future favor. This likely limits the willingness of others to work with them and limits their ability to log-roll. Long-term members too may be unlikely to mentor prospective citizen legislators or chose them as protégés since this effort would not have long-term pay-offs.

The lack of a long-term desire for a political career however may increase prospective legislators' effectiveness by decreasing their concern for reelection. Focusing on reelection is thought to make members less effective, and electoral security was another of Frantzich's approaches to understanding effectiveness. Frantzich (1979) notes that members with electoral security should be more effective because they have greater leeway to act as they wish and can spend less time seeking reelection. However, he found little support for his expectation that electoral security affects legislative effectiveness. Similarly, research examining members effectiveness after they plan to retire (free from electoral consideration) found retirees to be as effective (Lott 1990; Herrick, Moore, and Hibbing 1994; Rothenberg and Sanders 2000). Thus previous research seems to suggest that electoral considerations have little effect on members' effectiveness. We believe this to be the case because voters have little knowledge about what legislation a member introduces and members can "take credit," to use Mayhew's term, without seeing their legislation pass. When effectiveness is measured as more than seeing legislation passed, however, electoral considerations could have greater effects.

Measuring Legislative Behavior

To estimate the differences in the effectiveness of citizen and professional legislators we examined several indicators of members' activity and effectiveness. Three variables were used to measure activity levels. The first variable was the average number of bills and resolutions sponsored by members per congress in their first two congresses. Not included were bills and resolutions to which the member merely added his or her name as a co-sponsor. Often, co-sponsors simply attach their names to many bills as a sign of support. This does not signify the same magnitude of attachment to or work on legislation as being the primary sponsor. The second variable was the average number of amendments introduced per congress. Amendments differ from bills and resolutions in significant ways because they occur later in the legislative process. Amending activity indicates an effort to refine a debate already in progress, not to initiate the discussion. Data for both of these variables were collected from THOMAS, the Congressional website (http://thomas.loc.gov).[3] The third variable used to measure activity was members' average voting participation rates (percentage of time members cast votes on non-journal roll-call votes). A simple and visible way members can affect the passage of legislation is by casting votes on the legislation. These data came from CQ's Congressional Almanac (various years) and CQ Weekly Reports (various years).

Since we were not merely interested in levels of members' activities but also in their effectiveness, we examined three different ways members could be effective lawmakers: legislative effectiveness, media coverage, and committee assignments. First, to measure legislative effectiveness we estimated members' ability to get the legislation they introduced passed in the House. This is one of the clearest ways to be an effective legislator and the measure has been used elsewhere (Frantzich 1979; Hibbing 1991; Herrick, Moore, and Hibbing 1994). While some studies examined percent of legislation passed, others examined the number of pieces of legislation passed. We initially collected the number of bills, resolutions, and amendments. However, in both cases, a large number of members did not see any bill, resolution, or amendment they introduced pass in their first two congresses. As a result we created two dummy variables. The first one taps whether a member saw at least one bill or resolution pass (coded one, otherwise zero). The second variable taps whether a member saw at least one amendment pass (coded one, otherwise zero). These data were collected through THOMAS.[4]

The above measures define effectiveness as successfully shepherding legislation through the legislative process. However, a member may also be effective by having influence on the public debates or by being a spokesperson. To measure public influence we examined media coverage. Legislative debate increasingly occurs as much in the media as on the floor of the chamber. Media coverage also indicates the member's noteworthiness. Members with power and influence are likely to get more coverage. Media savvy even accords senators respect (Hibbing and Thomas 1990). For our measure of media coverage we collected the number of stories printed in the *Washington Post* that made a reference to a member in each congress of his/her first two congresses. The *Washington Post* was used since it has extensive coverage of House activities and is the primary local paper in the Capitol read by most Washington insiders.[5] We initially tried to limit the number of stories to those related to policy but found this to be an impossible task. For example, is a story mentioning how much money a member received from PACs a story on policy (campaign finance) or elections? Even stories completely unrelated to politics may indicate that the member is influential. An influential member appearing at a fundraiser, for example, is more newsworthy than the appearance of a less influential member. Here, we examined the average number of stories per congress.

A third way that members can affect policy debates involves committee assignment. Here, we used two measures. The first measure was whether a member has been assigned to a conference committee. Conference committees have considerable power, affecting the final version of a bill (Shepsle and Weingast 1987). In addition, members who are "players" on a bill are often assigned to the conference committee. Therefore, a member who was assigned to conference committees had greater influence than other members. To measure conference assignments we created a dummy variable for whether a member was assigned to any conference committees (coded one) or not (coded zero). The second measure was whether a member was assigned to a power committee. Certain committee assignments afford members greater power in the chamber than others. Following Deering and Smith (1997) the power committees included: Budget, Appropriations, Ways and Means, and Rules (coded one, otherwise zero). With these analyses we included those who won in special elections since length of service should have less influence on these variables.

Since many things can affect a member's effectiveness we used OLS or logistic regression to control for several factors. Logistic regression was used when the dependent variable was a dummy variable. First, we controlled for whether members were in the majority party. Members of the majority party have advantages in the legislative process and have more responsibility to introduce legislation (Frantzich 1979). While many of the early rational choice theories de-emphasized the role of parties in Congress, the conditional party government thesis espoused by Aldrich and Rohde (2000, 2001) predicts that parties influence policy outcomes when parties are polarized and homogeneous: two conditions present in the mid- and late 1990s. Thus, it seems reasonable to expect that members in the majority party, in the time period we examine, would be more effective and active than minority party members. Majority party status was measured by the number of congresses in which the member was in the majority party in their first two congresses. Since this variable was highly correlated with members' party (r=.80, p=.00) we did not include party in these analyses. We also examined variations in party support, assuming that members who were within the mainstream of their party should be more effective. For this measure we used members' average party unity scores over the first two congresses, corrected for nonattendance, as provided in *CQ Weekly Reports* (various years).

One may question whether or not the majority party will be more active when it is the Republican Party. The Republican Party, and its members, tend to favor smaller government and may want to see less legislation pass. We believe that in this time period they would have had an interest in being active and to decrease the size of government takes legislation. In fact, in the 104th Congress, Speaker Gingrich initiated the corrections calendar to facilitate the passage of legislation designed to correct existing laws and policies.

A third control is for whether members were in positions of power. Members with leadership positions are more active and effective than rank and file members (Frantzich 1979). Leaders have pressure put on them by groups to introduce legislation and have great resources to push their legislation through the House or get media coverage. Since the members we examined were in their first two congresses, none were committee chairs or party leader. Instead, we controlled for whether a member was assigned to a power committee. This control variable was not used when power committee assignment was the dependent variable.

Frantzich (1979) and others have also suggested that members' electoral security should affect their activity and effectiveness. We controlled for variation in members' electoral security by measuring the strength of their party in their districts. As in Chapters Three and Four, party strength was measured as percentage of the district's two-party vote going to the president's party in each member's district in 1992, 1996, and 2000. Electoral prospects may affect media coverage in other ways, as well. There is more electoral coverage of members running in close elections.

We also controlled for each member's progressive and intra-institutional ambition. Members with progressive ambition, the desire for higher office, tend to be more active but less successful than other members (Van Der Slik and Pernacciara 1979; Herrick and Moore 1993). Members with intra-institutional ambition tend to be less active but are more effective (Herrick and Moore 1993). Progressive ambition was coded one for members who sought a higher office, otherwise coded zero. Intra-institutional ambition was coded one if a member sought a leadership position, otherwise coded zero.

Two control variables were only used for analysis of media coverage. First, a variable was created for whether a member served on the Judiciary Committee during the congress President Clinton was impeached (coded one, otherwise coded zero). Members who were on the committee were quoted frequently during the impeachment procedure as this committee oversaw the process. Also, members representing Maryland and Virginia received more coverage than other members since these states border Washington, D.C. (coded one, otherwise coded zero).

Findings

There was no clear evidence that citizen legislators, retrospective or prospective, were more or less active than professional legislators (Table 5.1). Although prospective citizen legislators introduced fewer bills and resolutions and missed more votes, they were more likely to introduce amendments. However, none of these differences were statistically significant.[6] There was some evidence, however, that electoral concerns increase members' activity. Members who came from more secure districts introduced fewer bill amendments and cast fewer votes. Additionally, although retrospective citizen legislators introduced fewer bills and resolutions, and fewer amendments, they were more likely to cast their votes. But again none of the differences met normal levels of statistical significance. The model only did a moderate job predicting members' activity. The Adj. R^2 for bill and resolution introduction was only .09, and only two factors significantly affected the number of bills and resolutions members introduced: majority party and members' date of entry. The model was even less able to explain frequency of amendment introductions (Adj. $R^2=.02$), and only the level of members' party unity and electoral security were significantly related to amending activity. The model did a better job explaining the percentage of roll-call votes each member cast (Adj. $R^2=.14$).

The findings were mixed with regard to legislative effectiveness, seeing legislation introduced pass in the House. Prospective citizen legislators were significantly less successful seeing the bills and resolutions they introduce pass but were more likely to see amendments pass.[7] This last relationship neared normal levels of statistical significance. Since logistic coefficients are difficult to interpret, we calculated the probabilities that different types of legislators were successful in seeing their legislation pass. The average prospective professional leg-

Table 5.1. Citizen and Professional Legislators' Differences in Number of Bills, Resolutions, and Amendments Introduced and Voting Participation Rates

	Bill and Resolutions	Amendments	Voting
Prospective	-1.00	.49	-.45
	(1.37)	(.40)	(.40)
Retrospective	-.37	-.01	.07
	(.85)	(.25)	(.25)
Majority Party	1.68***	-.08	-.19
	(.61)	(.18)	(.18)
Party Unity	-.02	.04**	.01
	(.06)	(.02)	(.02)
Intra-institutional	-.03	-.11	-.03
	(1.33)	(.39)	(.39)
Progressive	.05	-.23	-.05
	(1.13)	(.33)	(.33)
Electoral Security	1.19	-.70***	-7.78***
	(4.75	(1.40)	(1.40)
Power Committee	.92	-.05	.14
	(1.09)	(.32)	(.32)
103rd Congress	-5.43**	.25	-.01
	(1.31)	(.39)	(.38)
104th Congress	-6.28***	.62+	.16
	(1.35)	(.40)	(.40)
105th Congress	-5.81***	-.14	-.70*
	(1.30)	(.39)	(.38)
Constant	14.24***	-2.26*	101.53***
	(4.37)	(1.29)	(1.28)
R^2	.13	.06	.17
Adj. R^2	.09	.02	.13
N	257	257	257

+< .20 * < .10 ** <.05 *** < .01 (using a two-tailed test)
Sources: *Almanac of American Politics* (various years), *CQ's Biographies of Freshman Members* (various years), *CQ's Politics in America 2002*, *CQ's Weekly Reports* (various years), and http://thomas.loc.gov. Data calculated by authors.
See Appendix A for explanation of the variables.

islator had a .26 probability of seeing a bill he introduced pass compared to .08 for the average citizen legislator.[8] With amendments, the probabilities were .52 and .70 respectively. The data too suggests that electoral concerns increase effectiveness. Members who came from safer districts were less likely to see the bills and amendments they introduce pass. Retrospective citizen legislators too were less able to see their bills and resolutions pass and more likely to see their amendments pass, but the relationships were noticeably smaller. For example, while the average retrospective professional legislator had a .26 probability of seeing a bill or resolution pass, the average retrospective citizen legislators had a .18 probability. The model did a moderate job explaining legislative success. The Cox and Snell pseudo-R^2s were .14 and .11.

The above analysis is limited, because it only looks at members' success at seeing legislation pass. Missing from this is members' ability to block legislation that is not desirable. Although citizen legislators may be at a disadvantage in seeing their legislation pass, they may be better at blocking legislation they dislike. Prospective citizen legislators, who are unconcerned about their future, may be willing to antagonize members to prevent legislations they dislike from passing. Former Rep. Tom Coburn (R-OK) demonstrates how prospective citizen legislators are free to accomplish their goals by being obstructionists. Since he planned to stay only six years, he was virtually unconcerned about building relationships and could take obstructionist measures to accomplish his goals. The key events during the budget debates in 1997 illustrate this view. During 1997, Coburn worked with several other conservative Republicans to try to push the leadership to work on a more conservative agenda. In March these members voted against the rule to bring up the leadership's bill to fund House committees. The most immediate cause of the problem was that the bill had a fourteen percent budget increase, but the action was also in response to general problems with the leadership (Koszczuk 1997; Gugliotta, *Washington Post*, April 1, 1997). Newt Gingrich, the Republican speaker, was so upset by the action that he forced these members to justify their votes during the Republican Caucus meeting, threatened their committee assignments, and encouraged them to leave the party (Koszczuk 1997, 679). In July, Coburn "derailed the Labor, Health and Human Services, and Education spending bill, blocking its floor consideration late in July by threatening dozens of amendments" (Greenblatt 1997, 1968). When the bill came up again in September, he, along with several other members, proposed one hundred amendments[10] designed to try to force the leadership to bring to the floor several conservative causes (Katz 1997; Katz and Nitschke 1997). These members were concerned that the leadership had made too many compromises with Democrats on the budget (Katz 1997; Katz and Nitschke 1997). Part of the reason obstructionism was successful was because the Republican Party had a small majority. According to Pianin and Eilperin (*Washington Post*, June 14, 1999):

Because the Republicans hold a bare six-vote majority in the House and can rarely depend on the minority Democrats for support, even a small handful of

Table 5.2. Logistic Regression Comparing Citizen and Professional Legislators' Likelihood of Passing Bills and Amendments

	Bills and Resolutions	Amendments
Prospective	-1.28***	.79+
	(.50)	(.56)
Retrospective	-.44+	.31
	(.31)	(.30)
Majority Party	1.13***	.06
	(.27)	(.21)
Party Unity	-.01	.06***
	(.02)	(.02)
Intra-institutional	-.06	.75+
	(.48)	(.54)
Progressive	.37	.30
	(.42)	(.42)
Electoral Security	-.20	-2.21+
	(1.68)	(1.67)
Power Committee	-.33	.40
	(.43)	(.40)
103rd Congress	-2.02***	-.20
	(.61)	(.47)
104th Congress	-2.44***	-.52
	(.66)	(.50)
105th Congress	-1.26**	-.72+
	(.60)	(.47)
Constant	1.23	-3.56**
	(1.55)	(1.58)
% predicted correctly	73.54	69.26
% predicted by mean	69.20	63.77
Improvement	4.34	5.49
Cox and Snell R^2	.14	.11
Nagelkerke R^2	.20	.15
Chi^2 (d.f.=11)	38.95***	30.07***
N	257	276

+< .20 * < .10 ** <.05 *** < .01 (using a two-tailed test)

Sources: *Almanac of American Politics* (various years), *CQ's Biographies of Freshman Members* (various years), *CQ's Politics in America 2002*, *CQ's Weekly Reports* (various years), and http://thomas.loc.gov. Data calculated by authors.

See Appendix A for explanation of the variables.

dissidents can frustrate Hastert [Speaker of the House] and his lieutenants. "If six people decide to get off the reservation, you've got a problem," said Rep. Ray LaHood (R-IL). "Any time six people get up in the morning and decide they don't like what the leadership is doing, we've got a problem."

Rep. Coburn's style alienated some members. The amendment filibuster upset the Republican leadership and several other members. In the Republican conference prior to the vote Rep. Dick Armey (R-TX), the majority leader, expressed considerable frustration with Coburn (Martinez 1999). Members from farm states believed Coburn was forcing their constituents to take bigger cuts than others (Greenblatt 1999). Or, as Church (1999) wrote in *CQ Weekly Report*, "Members of both parties denounced Coburn's effort. Republican Terry Everett of Alabama called Coburn's effort a 'self-righteous indulgence,' while Earl Pomeroy (D-ND), said members should know that 'hijacking the floor of this House is not the appropriate way to advance our convictions'" (*Congressional Record* 2005, 1272). One member even called him a "jerk" to his face (Coburn 2003, 153). However, he was relatively unconcerned about these responses. Because he signed and planned to keep the term limits pledge, there were few possible repercussions from the leadership. He said, "What are they going to do to you? You don't want a committee chairmanship. You're not looking for anything inside of Washington. You're looking to do for your constituents what you told them you would do" (Peaden and Herrick 2001).

There was little difference between citizen and professional legislators with regard to media coverage. Prospective citizen legislators had about one more story written about them than did prospective professional legislators.[10] Retrospective citizen and professional legislators had almost identical number of stories. The model, however, did a moderate job of predicting media mentions (R^2 =.18), with several of the variables being significantly related to media mentions. Three key variables related to media mentions were electoral security, living in Virginia or Maryland, and serving on the Judiciary Committee. That electoral security affected media coverage we believe says little about the importance of media coverage for reelection but that members running in close elections are newsworthy.

Prospective citizen legislators were less able to secure committee seats than were prospective professional legislators.[11] They were significantly less likely to gain a seat on a power committee, although they were slightly (insignificantly) more likely to gain a conference committee seat. Prospective professional legislators had a .20 probability of being assigned to a power committee compared to .07 for a citizen legislator. Thus, it appears as though party leaders do not want to "waste" a power committee seat on a member who will not be around long. There is evidence too that electoral security affects committee assignment. Members who come from safer districts were less likely to be assigned to power committees. This may be because the parties want to help electorally vulnerable members in their future elections. However, there was little evidence that lacking previous experience affected committee assignments. Retrospective citizen

Table 5.3. OLS Regression Comparing Citizen and Professional Legislators in Media Coverage

Prospective	.77
	(2.49)
Retrospective	-.02
	(1.54)
Majority Party	1.13
	(1.12)
Party Unity	.14+
	(.10)
Intra-institutional	4.19*
	(2.43)
Progressive	1.61
	(2.05)
Electoral Security	-17.76**
	(8.75)
Power Committee	-2.30
	(2.00)
103rd Congress	.54
	(2.39)
104th Congress	4.41*
	(2.46)
105th Congress	.26
	(2.39)
VA/MD	21.51***
	(4.80)
Judiciary Committee	18.49***
	(4.27)
Constant	6.37
	(8.03)
R^2	.22
Adj. R^2	.18
N	256

+< .20 * < .10 ** <.05 *** < .01 (using a two-tailed test)
Data sources: *Almanac of American Politics* (various years), *CQ's Biographies of Freshman Members* (various years), *CQ's Politics in America 2002*, *CQ's Weekly Reports* (various years), and Lexis-Nexis. Data calculated by authors.
See Appendix A for explanation of the variables.

Table 5.4. Logistic Regression Comparing Citizen and Professional Legislators in Committee Assignments

	Power Committee	Conference Committee
Prospective	-1.30**	.23
	(.65)	(.46)
Retrospective	.20	.16
	(.39)	(.28)
Majority Party	.05	.10
	(.26)	(.20)
Party Unity	.05*	.00
	(.03)	(.02)
Intra-institutional	.69	.51
	(.66)	(.47)
Progressive	.70+	-.02
	(.52)	(.38)
Electoral Security	-9.35**	-2.45+
	(3.25)	(1.62)
Power Committee	—	.82**
		(.37)
103rd Congress	-10.20	1.14***
	(16.34)	(.44)
104th Congress	-.40	.25
	(.49)	(.45)
105th Congress	-.78+	.32
	(.48)	(.43)
Constant	-.27	.54
	(2.38)	(1.46)
% predicted correctly	84.05	61.48
% predicted by mean	78.26	55.80
Improvement	5.79	5.68
Cox and Snell R^2	.26	.08
Nagelkerke R^2	.41	.10
Chi^2	78.39***(10 d.f.)	20.48**(11 d.f.)
N	257	257

+< .20 * < .10 ** <.05 *** < .01 (using a two-tailed test)

Sources: *Almanac of American Politics* (various years), adaction.org, *CQ's Biographies of Freshman Members* (various years), *CQ's Politics in America 2002, CQ's Weekly Reports* (various years), and http://thomas.loc.gov. Data calculated by authors. See Appendix A for explanation of the variables.

legislators were slightly more likely to gain both power and conference committee seats, but the differences were quite small and not statistically significant.

While the above analysis was limited to looking at powerful committee seats, the case studies offer some evidence that party leadership was not limited to professional legislators. One prospective citizen legislator was able to gain a party leadership position: Former Rep. Tillie Fowler (R-FL). As a freshman, she gained her first leadership position as Co-chair of the Freshmen Republican Reform Task Force. However, her main leadership position was Vice-chair of the Republican Conference. Although she arrived on Capitol Hill after promising to limit her length of service, she had previous political experience. Even though she was able to gain a leadership position, her term limits pledge may have been an obstacle. There were some reports that she told the party she would break her pledge to gain the position (Brainerd 1999, 1444). However, she asserts that though some people asked if she would break her pledge she said she planned to leave in two years and "was going to work hard those two years and do what [she] could do for the Conference" (Fowler 2004). Although being a prospective citizen legislator likely made it more difficult to become a leader, we believe that since she had experience and was a moderate reformer, she was able to reach both camps.[12] Former Rep. Fowler was committed to term limits and reform, but was not part of the radical class of 1994 and was not an obstructionist. Additionally, she said "I was fortunate since I was a staffer on this Hill. I hit the ground running, my learning curve was not as sharp as a lot of new members so that helps me tremendously" (Fowler 2004). In an interview she said there were two types of reformers seeking to change the institution. She characterized herself as a reformer seeking to build up the institution, while other reformers sought to tear it down (Fowler 2004).

Conclusion

The analysis generally finds a greater difference between prospective citizen and professional legislators than between retrospective citizen and professional legislators. However, the difference may be more of a style than degree. Prospective citizen legislators had a difficult time seeing the legislation they introduced pass or being assigned to a power committee, but that did not prevent some from being able to block the legislation they viewed negatively. How generalizable the findings are with regard to blocking legislation is debatable. Given the small majority held by the Republicans the ability of any member to block the passage of legislation was enhanced. It only took a handful of majority members voting against the party to prevent a bill from passing. The evidence also suggests that electoral considerations may affect effectiveness. Members coming from safe districts were less likely to get good committee assignments, less likely to see their legislation pass and less likely to introduce amendments and cast votes. This offers some support for the idea that electoral concerns increase rather than decrease effectiveness. Members need to be active and effective to win votes, and the parties through committee assignments want to help them win. Finally, there is little evidence that previous expérience is essential to being an effective legislator.

These findings have some implication for representation. If citizens want a member who will be able to stop legislation from passing, then a prospective citizen legislator may be able to provide greater representation of their preferences. However, if citizens want a member who will be able to enact legislation that will advance their interests, then a professional legislator would be preferred. The findings also suggest that competitive elections or meaningful elections may increase members' effectiveness. However, we have no direct evidence of why electorally insecure members were more effective. It may be that they work harder, in which case citizens who want legislators who will work hard and be able to enact legislation should prefer professional legislators. However, if they were more effective because their party helped them out in order to improve their electoral prospects, then competitive elections would not increase productivity as it is unlikely a party would be able to assist all members.

Notes

1. The other three theories concerned electoral security, leadership, and power.

2. They had similar findings with regard to effectiveness, i.e., experienced members were statistically significantly more effective, but substantively the difference was small.

3. We collected this data by searching for each member within the bill summary and status cite.

4. We counted a bill or amendment as passed if it passed in the House regardless of what happened in the Senate.

5. To identify stories we searched in Lexis-Nexis to find sentences that included the member's last names and the term "Rep." First names were used when more than one member had the same last name or there was reason to suspect that a sentence could have a word that is a member's last name, e.g., the last name was also a common noun. First names were not used all the time because some members used nicknames some but not all of the time. The search was done congress by congress (1995 and 1996, for example, were examined for the 104th Congress).

6. When all members who signed the pledge were considered to be prospective citizen legislators, there were no significant differences from those reported. Appendix B suggest that the conclusions would be the same had the citizen legislator category excluded those exhibiting progressive ambition; however, the difference with regard to amending may have been stronger.

7. When all members who signed the pledge were considered to be prospective citizen legislators, the relationship between being a prospective citizen legislators and success with amendments no longer neared statistical significance. Appendix B suggests that the conclusions would be the same had the citizen legislator category excluded those exhibiting progressive ambition.

8. This was calculated from the logistic equation and assumes the member entered in the 106th Congress, was in the majority party one year, had 60 percent for party strength, and had a 90 percent on the party unity. The member also did not serve on a power committee or had progressive or intra-institutional ambition.

9. The number of amendments we identified that were officially introduced by Coburn was much smaller. This was because, although the amendments were drafted, they were never officially introduced.

10. When all members who signed the pledge were considered to be prospective citizen legislators, the relationship changed directions but remained statistically insignificant. Appendix B suggests that the conclusions would be the same had the citizen legislator category excluded those exhibiting progressive ambition.

11. When all members who signed the pledge were considered to be prospective citizen legislators there were not significant differences from those reported. Appendix B suggests that the conclusions would be the same had the citizen legislator category excluded those exhibiting progressive ambition.

12. She has been characterized as a moderate, soft-spoken, and a close advisor to Speaker Hastert (Giroux et al. 2000, 56).

Chapter Six
Ethics

Political power gives representatives the ability to promote good public policy for their constituents, and it also offers opportunities to promote policies to advance their own interests. To offer quality substantive representation, members need to advocate their constituents' interests, not their own personal interests or those of their campaign donors. As such, to be more effective representatives, citizen legislators need to be more ethical than professional legislators. Whatever the reality, people expect that citizen legislators will be more ethical than professional legislators (Armor 1994; Jacob 1994; Petracca 1992, 23-24). They argue that the longer people are politicians, the more likely they are to be caught up in the trappings of the office and come to expect special treatment or compromise their principles. According to Paul Jacob, "If you stay in power for a very long period of time, you're going to be more and more tempted to sacrifice principle on the altar of political convenience" (http://www.termlimits.org /Press/Common_Sense/cs977.html). Mark Sanford (R-SC), who signed the term limits pledge, expressed concern about the deference and privilege paid to representatives and senators when relating the story of military officers straining out ice-cubes by hand from a glass of lemonade at Sen. Strom Thurmond's (R-SC) request (Sanford 2000, 4-5).

We are skeptical of the argument that long service or the desire for it necessarily causes unethical behaviors. Instead, we believe that citizen legislators are as likely, or even more likely, to behave unethically. Citizen legislators lack an understanding of legislative ethics, have more potential conflicts of interest and may suffer fewer consequences if caught. In this chapter we look at two ways citizen and professional legislators may differ in their ethics. First, we examine whether citizen legislators are less likely to violate the ethics rules than professional legislators. Second, we examine whether citizen legislators are less likely to have conflicts of interest. The next chapter examines members' relationships with special interest groups. Although these relationships can be unethical, we discuss them in a separate chapter because they do necessary have to be unethical.

Are Citizen Legislators Less Likely to Violate the Official Ethics Standards?

Initially we conceptualized legislative ethics in a legalistic way, allowing laws and codes of ethical conduct to decide what is unethical. When members violate the House Code of Conduct (Appendix C) or the law, they are behaving unethically. This conceptualization has been criticized because it is atheoretical. It is not based on any notions of what makes some behaviors inappropriate for legislators. Another way to conceptualize ethics for legislators is based on democratic ideals (Heywood 1997). It suggests that there is an absolute ethical standard; those behaviors that harm the democratic processes are by definition unethical. These two definitions are not mutually exclusive, since the House rules are related to democratic principles. In fact, work examining House ethics notes that the ethics rules—while being far from perfect—address problems likely to harm the legislative process (Herrick 2003; Thompson 1995). For example, rules limiting the ability of members to accept gifts or honorariums from interest groups help to limit the ability of members to work for interest groups to better themselves instead of their constituents.

Noting that the ethics rules are related to democratic and legislative principles illuminates their importance to representation. Thompson (1995) identifies three principles of legislative ethics: 1) independence (making decisions based on merit); 2) accountability (maintaining the public's confidence in Congress); and 3) fairness (assuming that everyone plays by the same rules and that the rules are fair). Independence clearly relates to representation since basing decisions on merit implies that members make decisions based on the interests of the constituents or other legitimate interests. These other interests could include the nations' interest or Congress's institutional interests or conceivably others. However, when members make decisions based on things other than the merits of a policy they are not making them in the interests of constituents. The accountability principle relates to representation in a different way. By maintaining public confidence in the legislative body, legislators can increase the likelihood that citizens will participate in the process. Democratic institutions are dependent on the public's willingness to voluntarily comply with laws, to pay taxes, and to vote. Governments have the ability to coerce such behavior but to do so is inefficient and diminishes governments' legitimacy (Tyler 1990). Consequently, when members' actions diminish the public's confidence, they hurt democracy and the representational nature of Congress. The fairness principle, too, relates to representation. It requires that members "fulfill their obligations to colleagues, staff, challengers, other officials, and the institution as a whole" (Thompson 1995, 22). If the system is not fair, then some interests will be less likely to receive representation than others. If elections give certain types of people an advantage, then descriptive representation may be harmed because some groups are not reflected in the legislature. If some members have unfair advantages in the processes, then some constituents get more and others less substantive representation. Thus, the chamber itself is less representative of constituents' interests.

The small amount of research that empirically examines what contributes to the likelihood that members violate ethics rules can be used to predict that professional legislators will be more ethical than citizen legislators. Recent work finds that opportunity, costs, and propensity for violating the rules increase such violations (Herrick 2003, 98-105). First, some members have greater opportunities to violate the standards because they are in positions of power. Members in positions of power, such as leaders and those of the majority party, have more to offer political actors wanting a special favor, including those willing to violate rules to get those favors. Stewart (1994) found that members in the majority party were more likely to have been involved in the 1992 House Banking Scandal, although he did not find any difference between committee leaders and non-leaders. Second, members may vary in their propensity to violate the standards. Members who have greater needs, such as those with little wealth, those that lack strong party supporters and those who are young are more likely to violate the standards (Herrick 2003). Third, members likely to incur great costs if caught are less likely to violate the standards. Herrick (2003) finds that members who have progressive ambition, highly-educated constituents, and run in close elections are less likely to violate the ethical standard than other members. Opportunity, costs, and propensity are related to ambition/reelection and experience debates.

This model does not predict that citizen legislators will be less likely than professional legislators to violate the standards. If, as we have assumed, citizen legislators, particularly prospective citizen legislators, have less political ambition, they are likely to have fewer costs associated with violating the standards. If a citizen legislator is caught up in a scandal that limits or ruins his/her political career, the member has not incurred a cost because that was not something desired. Of course, people also avoid scandals to prevent embarrassment, hurting family and friends, and out of a desire to do what is right. We doubt these conditions significantly differ between citizen and professional legislators. Although supporters of citizen legislators often assume that professional legislators are unethical because their experiences as politicians corrupt them, there is little evidence to support such a blanket statement. The vast majority of long-serving members have behaved ethically, and several long-serving members who have violated ethics had histories of questionable behavior. For example, prior to running for the House, Rep. Jim Traficant (R-OH), who was expelled from the House in 2003, had been indicated after being taped accepting bribes when he was sheriff in 1983 (Leibovich, *Washington Post*, October 27, 2002).

Instead of being more ethical, retrospective citizen legislators' lack of political experience may make them less understanding of the rules or the reasons behind them. Those who lack experience may have less understanding of why the ethical standards exist and are necessary. Acceptable behavior in the private sphere is often unacceptable in a legislature (Thompson 1995). For example, it is fine to work for your own financial betterment in the private sector, but that is not the case in the public sector. Even if citizen legislators are motivated to serve out of a desire to pursue specific public policies and not for personal goals, they still may have a propensity to violate ethical standards. Advocates of political causes have been known to engage in unethical behaviors to advance those causes. Oliver North, for example, is reported to have violated laws and sold weapons to Iran in order to help the Contras (Fried 1997, 62-73).

The third part of the model is opportunity, and citizen legislators should have roughly the same opportunity as others. Although it is often thought that citizen legislators are less likely to garner leadership positions, we found that retrospective citizen legislators were slightly more likely to be assigned to power committees and prospective citizen legislators were less likely to be (see Chapter Five). There are no reasons to expect that citizen legislators would be more or less likely to belong to the majority party; however, citizen legislators, retrospective and prospective, in our population were more likely to be Republicans and thus in the majority.

To determine whether citizen legislators, defined as either retrospective or prospective, were less likely to have violated the ethics standards, we used two measures. First, we examined whether members had been officially accused of violating ethics standards or the law. To do this we used the *Washington Post*, *CQ Weekly Reports*, and *CQ Almanacs* (all various years).[2] Second, we examined whether members violated ethics standards. To do this, we determined whether the Committee on the Standards of Official Conduct found that a member had violated the standards (even if a member was not punished for doing so), been found guilty in a court of law, or admitted wrongdoing.[3] We examined both accusations and convictions, because both have biases. Since the House is reluctant to convict members and are unable to if the member resigns before action is taken, convictions probably are an undercount (Thompson 1995; Herrick 2003). Using only the number of accusations, on the other hand, leads to an over-count of violations since some members are wrongly accused of inappropriate behavior.

These data indicate citizen legislators, regardless of definition, were more likely to have been accused of and/or found guilty of some ethical breach.[4] While 10.7 percent of the prospective citizen legislators were accused of violating the standards, only 3.4 percent of the other legislators faced such accusations. Retrospective citizen legislators were also more likely to have been accused than others. While 7.4 percent of the retrospective citizen legislators were accused of a violation, just 1.2 percent of the other legislators were accused. Using ANOVA, both differences were statistically significant at the .10 level. The evidence also suggests that both types of citizen legislators were more likely to be found guilty of violating the rules. Just over 3.5 percent of the prospective citizen legislators were found guilty compared to just 1.4 of the other members. Also 2.7 percent of the retrospective citizen legislators were found guilty, compared to .6 percent of the other members. In the case of conviction the differences were not statistically significant according to the ANOVA analysis. This is likely due to the small number of convictions. Thus, both types of citizen legislators were more likely to have violated the stated standards than were other members. Although bivariate analyses are often suspect, we did not perform multivariate analysis because the number of cases was too small. Just thirteen members had been accused and only five were found guilty of wrongdoing.

Do Citizen Legislators have Greater Conflicts of Interest than do Professional Legislators?

As noted earlier, citizen legislators are expected to have greater conflicts of interest than other members. Usually, conflicts of interest are thought to occur when members personally benefit from their official position. Although this gain is often financial, it can be anything, including political or sexual. We expected citizen legislators to be more likely to have conflicts of interest because they are more closely connected to the private sector through the careers they had prior to assuming public office. Examples are Bob Riley, who had a long career in agriculture and small business and served on the Agriculture and the Banking and Financial Services committees, and Mark Sanford, who had a career in real estate and financial investing and served on the joint economic committee. We have found no evidence that these legislators made decisions specifically to advance their own interests, however, the situations do create the possibility of self-serving votes—real or not. Not only are citizen legislators who came directly from the private sphere likely to have conflicts of interest, but so too are prospective citizen legislators. Prospective citizen legislators are more likely to make decisions that could affect their future livelihood. They may know they are likely to return to a profession and make decisions that aid that profession. Additionally, since they are less interested in a political career, elections will be less likely to constrain their behaviors or tie them to the constituents.

We identified four types of conflicts of interest faced by the members. In some ways the conflicts are not unique to citizen legislators, but the context of their conflicts are unique. One of the conflicts relates to the ban on fiduciary relationships, i.e., relationships that make members obligated to others. The House banned fiduciary relationships primarily to prevent lawyers from working on legislation to aid their clients, but it has been applied to other professions. When Dr. Coburn arrived on Capitol Hill, he asked the ethics committee if he would violate the rules by continuing to practice medicine during his time in office.[5] The committee's response did not address the fiduciary issue. Rather it only explained how he could stay within the outside earnings limit. Two years later, when another doctor, Rep. Victor F. Snyder (D-AR), asked for a similar ruling, he was told that he could not charge for his services because of the fiduciary rule. Coburn complained about the ruling. He was concerned that it would force him to stop practicing medicine, because he could not afford insurance or a nurse without charging for his services (Romano, *Washington Post*, January 23, 1998; Coburn 2003, 180-83). Coburn threatened to quit over the issue, but then a compromise was worked out so that he could continue his medical practice. The issue was particularly important to Coburn because as a citizen legislator he wished to return to his practice full time when he left Congress. Other members who have to leave their job to serve in the House but do not plan to return to the job in a few years do not face the same dilemma as did Coburn. Although Coburn may be right that his relationship with his patients is unlikely to involve "influence peddling," his working as a doctor while in office still may not be in the best interests of his constituents overall. He had to divide his attention between two jobs, something most employers frown upon. By all accounts, Coburn worked hard as a member of Congress, and one might wonder how much more he could have done for his constituents had he spent that time on legislative matters, visiting with constituents, or even resting to get ready for another week on the Hill, instead of devoting that time to his medical practice.[6]

A second type of ethical concern is when members make decisions that can affect their livelihood. Again, Coburn is a case in point. While in office, Coburn made several policy decisions that could affect his medical practice, a practice he not only planned to return to but one he continued while in office. Healthcare and abortion were key issues during his time in Congress, and, as an obstetrician, his line of work was affected by these decisions. In office, he and Rep. John Shadegg (R-AZ) co-authored a patients' bill of rights bill that affected HMOs and the degree to which HMOs were free to go against doctors' recommendations for treatment. Also in 2000, Coburn was able to vote on legislation giving doctors the opportunity to unionize and to increase the budget for Medicare because earlier cuts had hurt rural and midsized hospitals (Vita, *Washington Post*, October 3, 2000). These are hospitals Coburn would use in his practice. Throughout his political career, he was active in other medical issues, such as abortion, HIV, and prescription drug subsidies, all likely to affect his medical practice. Coburn was aware of the conflicts of interest and in at least one situation did not vote because of conflicts of interest. When this happened, however, constituents lost their representation.

Although a professional politician, Rep. Frank Lucas (R-OK) faces a similar conflict of interest. He owns a working ranch and sits on the Agricultural Committee. Although the House rules allow farmers to maintain their farms, it is inconsistent with the limits on outside earnings (Coburn 2003, 183). Lucas is involved in numerous decisions that could affect his business. While this conflict poses many of the same issues as Coburn's conflict, there is a difference. Coburn only faced his voters twice as an incumbent while Lucas has faced his voters five times and will again for the foreseeable future. This means that his interest in reelection is more likely to constrain his behavior. Legislators also are asked to vote on issues affecting their legislative careers, such as term limits, campaign finance, and congressional pay raises. However, since these members must face reelection, there is a check on their behaviors. But members disinterested or unable to seek reelection do not have this check.

A third conflict of interest involves investments. According to a *Washington Post* article, Rep. Sue Kelly (R-NY) and three other members of the House Financial Services subcommittee either owned stock, or their spouses owned stock, in Fannie Mae or Freddie Mac (Johnson and Day, June 18, 2003). Although one member of the subcommittee overseeing Fannie Mae and Freddie Mac recused himself, Rep. Kelly stated that she would not.[7] Two other members on the committee had similar conflicts, both of whom did not publicly state if they would recuse themselves. One of the other members had previous political experience, Rep. Judy Biggert (R-IL), and the other did not, Rep. Carolyn McCarthy (D-NY). In this case, previous political experience was unrelated to whether members had conflicts of interest or how they reacted to them. Regardless of previous experience, members had the conflict and were reluctant to recuse themselves.

The fourth conflict of interest involves working on behalf of a campaign donor. Professional legislators are usually thought to be more prone to these problems because of the need for reelection (Coburn 2003). Rep. Kelly, incurred this type of problem when Rep. Jerrold Nadler (D-NY) accused Kelly of helping Donald Trump after receiving campaign donations from him. The issue involved transportation money being spent to move a highway that blocked Trump's view of the Hudson River. Kelly, however, stated that her decision to support moving the highway was to insure a greenway along the Hudson River (Eilperin, *Washington Post*, August 6, 1998). Whether Rep. Kelly purposely worked to aid a large donor is less important than the appearance that she did as this appearance affects the accountability principle.

Conclusion

The findings of this chapter suggest that citizen legislators are not immune from ethical conflicts and violations. Citizen legislators, defined as prospective or retrospective, were more likely to have been accused and convicted of unethical behaviors. Additionally, the conflicts we found in our qualitative analysis suggest that citizen legislators face numerous ethical conflicts. The lack of experience and understanding of the Hill may in part explain the differences. Equally important may be that they want to stay active in their professions and that they have fewer electoral checks on their decisions. These findings do not indicate that citizen legislators are more likely to make decisions that improve independence, fairness, or accountability. All of these characteristics are important for members to offer high quality representation to their constituents. In this chapter, we focused on violation of the House rules and conflicts of interests. In the next chapter we look at another issue that relates to ethics, which is members' relationships with interest groups.

Notes

1. In addition to this code there are several laws and other rules that limit members' behavior. For a complete list, see the *Ethics Manual for Members, Officers, and Employees of the U.S. House of Representatives* (www.house.gov/ethics).

2. In the *Washington Post* we searched for "ethics" and members' names. In the CQ publications we looked up the articles on congressional ethics.

3. Sometimes the committee will find that a member did violate the rules but might not recommend an official condemnation. This may occur because the accused member may have already made some restitution or the violation was minor. It may also occur for political reasons.

4. When all members who signed the pledge were considered to be prospective citizen legislators, the conclusions were the same. Appendix B shows that, if anything, the findings would have been stronger had the citizen legislator category excluded those exhibiting progressive ambition,

5. Since entering the Senate in 2005, Coburn has continued to have this conflict.

6. In his book, Coburn (2003) is critical of the ruling that he cannot use his name in his practice. However, to do so may give him greater name recognition and increase the desire of potential patients to want a congressman doctor. In essence, his legislative work is an advertisement for his medical practice and vice-versa.

7. The member who recused himself had been on the board of Freddie Mac.

Chapter Seven
Interest Group Relations

A common concern with professional legislators is that they are too responsive to special interests. According to the 1994 National Elections Study, approximately 76 percent of Americans thought government officials focused on big interests and not the people (http://umich.edu/~nes/nesguide/toptable/tab5a_2 .htm).[1] Even though Americans' attitudes toward government have improved over the past ten years, 56 percent still felt that way in 2004 (http://umich.edu /~nes/nesguide/toptable/tab5a_2.htm). Because election costs continue to escalate, and because interest groups, through political action committees (PACs), are an important funding source, it may not be surprising that Americans perceive elected officials as beholden to special interests. This is an inherent problem for professional politicians since they are assumed to be reelection-focused:

> The present situation is that members have already sold out to the special interests in order to keep their present jobs forever. Limits [term limits] will put in office people who are less beholden to the special interests, ones who know that Congress will not be their entire lives, ones who know that there was life before Congress and there will be life afterwards. Such congressmen will be less likely to sell out to the special interests (Armor 1994, 99).

Members focused on their political careers will do anything for reelection, including accepting money from special interests and working on their behalf while ignoring constituent concerns. Another way that long service can increase members' ties to interest groups is through the cozy relationships or iron triangles that develop between long serving members and the interests they regulate.[2] Finally, many criticize professional politicians for becoming a part of the Washington environment, fearing that they are concerned about what goes on inside the Capitol to the detriment of those at home. This environment distances and isolates members from their districts and makes members feel superior to their constituents. This environment is also thought to advantage special interests. The concern that interest groups have too much influence on members may be legitimate. Since many issues are not salient to the majority of voters, members have considerable leeway to work on issues unrelated to their constituents' interests. The empirical research on interest group influence on Congress suggests that interest groups have more effect on members' behavior early in the legislative process than during the floor voting stage. Research examining the effects of PAC contributions and lobbying on members' roll-call behavior has been mixed. A few studies, such as Haider-Markel's (1999) examination of gay-related roll-call votes, find that PAC campaign contributions and interest group lobbying efforts had some affect on members' votes. However, most research has found little effect of group activity on members' roll-call votes (Grenzke 1989; Wright 1985). There is more evidence, however, that interest groups play a role in members' behavior at the committee stage of the legislative process. Lobbying and PAC contributions have been found to affect members' votes in committee (Wright 1990) as well as members' levels of participation (Hall and Wayman 1990). This is also a stage that is typically less visible to the public. Still, one needs to be careful not to overstate the influence of groups. Evans's (1996) examination of group influence on two committees concludes that although interest groups were successful more times than not, under certain conditions, particularly when there was conflict between groups, they were unsuccessful in getting what they wanted from committees.

The degree to which interest group activity affects members' legislative behaviors subsequently alters the degree of representation. One could argue that members' ties to interest groups do not hurt members' ability to represent their constituents. The pluralist theory after all argues that interest groups represent the people's interests to the government. Also if a member's constituents are not directly affected by policy concerns, then voting for these concerns does not harm constituent representation. On the other hand, it may divert members' attention and time away from working on policies more directly tied to their constituents. Also, in the absence of perfect equality of resources and skills across groups, some interests will exert disproportionate influence.

Even if interest groups do not influence members, their association with groups may still be problematic. Being dependent on interest groups, especially for campaign funds, harms the accountability principle of legislative ethics. The accountability principle requires members to act in ways that build or maintain the public's confidence in the legislative process (Thompson 1995). Close interest group ties harm the accountability principle, because the public believes that special and moneyed interests have so much sway in Washington that members lose touch with the people (Hibbing and Theiss-Morse 1995). Whether members are influenced by special interests is less important than the perception that they are influenced, since the perception lowers the public's approval of Congress. Thus, anything members do that reinforces the perception of a Congress dependent on special interests violates this principle.

We do not believe that citizen legislators are more or less likely to develop ties with interest groups than are professional legislators. To understand whether citizen or professional legislators are less likely to develop ties with interest groups requires some understanding of the logic behind the relationship between interest groups and legislators and how this relates to political experience and ambition. If we understand members and groups as rational actors, interest groups will associate with members if it benefits them, and members will associate with interest groups if it benefits them. Thus, PACs give money to candidates likely to win, who have power in the areas of their interest, and who share their concerns. Groups will also try to minimize the costs associated with their work, such as lobbying their legislative friends. That is, they put pressure on those who support their cause instead of lobbying members opposed to their cause who are unlikely to change. Little research has been done to see which groups members are likely to work with, or if they will work with them at all. But presumably members who see it in their advantage to associate with a particular group will associate with that group. Based on this view, citizen legislators will be less likely to associate with interest groups if they do not see it in their interests to do so and/or if interest groups are less likely to see it in their interests to associate with them.

On the one hand, citizen legislators are likely to have incentives to build ties with interest groups. If citizen legislators are motivated to serve to pursue specific policy goals, they may see value in working with these groups to advance their shared policy goals. Because of their private sector careers, citizen legislators may even have close ties to some groups before entering the House. For example, farmers who are elected to Congress are likely to be members of farming groups such as the Farm Bureau. Furthermore, retrospective citizen legislators may be more dependent on groups for information because the have less information when they enter the House. Information, both policy and political, is a valuable commodity that interest groups offer legislators. The lack of knowledge in policy areas is most likely a problem for members who enter Congress without previous experience. Such members are unlikely to have had the opportunity to develop the kind of policy expertise or familiarity with the variety of issues that policy makers have developed.

Prospective citizen legislators are likely to have other reasons for having close relationships with interest groups. Most notably, they may be thinking about what they will do when they leave Congress. Rep. Tim Roemer (D-IN), for example explains:

> Term limits will also create the potential hazards that more Members of Congress will favor special interests as their term of service expires and they look forward to their next career. In this vein, Alexander Hamilton argued that term limits would tempt "ignoble views" by office holders who would have thought about nothing else than what their next job would be rather than focusing on the people's business (*Congressional Record* 1995, H3925).

In essence, prospective citizen legislators may be encouraged to build relationships with interests in order to secure a job when they leave Congress.

On the other hand, if we assumed the desire for reelection drives the connection between legislators and special interests, it is possible that citizen legislators could have fewer electoral incentives to engage with groups. If the strength of the desire for reelection is related to the amount of PAC money members receive, and if citizen legislators are less reelection driven, then they may seek fewer PAC dollars. Rep. Bill McCollum (R-FL) stated:

> The fact of the matter is that only if we limit the length of time somebody can serve in the House and Senate will we take away what has become the compelling reason about this place for all too many of us, and that is to try to get reelected, to spend time pleasing every interest group, every faction, as James Madison would call it, in order to be sure that the next time around we will get back to coming back to Washington again to serve and stay here for that length of time (*Congressional Record* 1995, H 2329).

The relationship between an interest group and a legislator runs two ways. Each must have something of value to offer the other. If citizen legislators have incentives to build relationships with interest groups but interest groups lack incentives to work with citizen legislators, then a relationship between the two is unlikely. There are two factors that could minimize the incentives interest groups have to build relationships with citizen legislators. First, interest groups may not see long-term benefits to building relationships with prospective citizen legislators. They may work with members for a given bill but see little incentive to build long-term relationships, since members will be leaving within a fairly short time period. Second, if interest groups are more interested in building relationships with members in power and if citizen legislators are less likely to have or gain power, then they may see little incentive to build relationships with these members. Conversely, they may see retrospective citizen legislators as more open to influence, since they may lack a track record on their policy concerns and be more likely to work with them.

Based on the above, it is unclear whether citizen or professional legislators will have stronger relationships with interest groups. If citizen legislators are less concerned about reelection than are professional legislators, then there is little reason to expect them to develop ties to PACs. However, if citizen legislators are concerned with advancing a specific legislative agenda, then it is reasonable to assume that a citizen legislator will develop ties with interest groups who work on that agenda. Also, retrospective citizen legislators may be more dependent on interest groups for more information while prospective citizen legislators may work with groups to gain post-congressional jobs.

Citizen Legislators' Ties with Groups

To estimate members' ties with interest groups we used three measures. Each relates to a unique need that could be satisfied by interest groups. First, we examined PAC campaign contributions. A common concern expressed by clean government groups is that members become beholden to interests because they receive large campaign donations from them. Even if these donations do not buy members' votes, they are thought to buy access to members. These data came from *Open Secrets* (http://www.opensecrets.org), a website operated by the Center for Responsive Politics. *Open Secrets* did not give information about members' elections if they lost their reelection bid. In these cases we collected the data from the Federal Elections Commission website (http://www.fec.gov). We examined these data in two different forms. One was total amount of money raised from PACs and the other was the percentage of money raised by a member that came from PACs. We felt it necessary to look at both percentages and total dollars raised, because each measure has its own biases. Looking at percentages masks large donations from PACs. For example, a member could raise $250,000 from PACs but it could be a relatively small percentage if the member raised several million dollars. Conversely, a member could have accepted a small dollar amount from PACs because his/her reelection costs were small, but nevertheless relied heavily upon PACs for his/her reelection. We examined campaign contributions instead of independent expenditures, since they were given directly to the candidate. We examined members' first two election cycles separately, because the competitiveness of a member's race varies from election to election, and the competitiveness of a race affects how much campaign money members' need. For this analysis, we include all members with available information who were not elected in a special election.

OLS regression was used to control for several variables likely to affect how much money members raised. First, we controlled for two factors related to the competitiveness of the race: percent of vote the member received in the election and total amount of money raised. The data for percent of vote came from *CQ Weekly Reports* (various years), and data for money raised came from *Open Secrets*, and the Federal Election Commission (FEC). We also controlled for factors that might affect whether PACs were likely to contribute to the campaign. These included party, majority party status, and party unity scores. Generally, Republicans were expected to raise more money than Democrats. Members belonging to the majority party were likely to raise more money than those in the minority, and those who were more ideologically moderate (low party unity scores) raised more money than those who were ideologically extreme. For these measures we included the data for the relevant congress, that is, we included scores from the first congress for the equation from the first congress. One exception to this was that in members' second reelection bid we used the number of congresses that a member was in the majority, instead of just whether the member was in the majority in the second congress.[3] We believe there could be some carry over effects on PACs if a member was in the majority party in the previous term.

Second, we examined whether members became lobbyists when they retired from the House. It is feared that members looking past their time in office develop close relationships with groups to land lucrative post-congressional lobbying jobs. To estimate which members land these jobs, we determined which of our members who have left the House have registered as lobbyists with the Clerk of the House. This measure may undercount actual lobbyists since some may not have to register, either because their job does not technically fit the legal definition of lobbying or former members lobby at the state or local level. Nevertheless, those who registered were assumed to have had close ties with the group during their tenure in the House. In examining this group of members we look at those who left the House prior 2003, and have spent some time out of elective office since leaving the House. Those who left since 2003 may have not had enough time to find a lobbying job and register, and those who won other elective office cannot become lobbyists. This left us 105 cases. In this analysis, we used logistic regression to control for party, age, and when the member left office. Other controls were considered, such as relationships with interest groups (PAC money, honorarium, or trips) or power in the chamber (power committee and bills and resolutions passed), but they were not significantly related to whether members became lobbyists and did not affect the relationship between our citizen legislator variables and whether members became lobbyists.

Finally, we measured the contact members had with interest groups while in office. To do this we examined the number of junkets and amount of honorarium. In 1995, Congress passed legislation to ban trips but it did allow groups to offer fact-finding trips and speaking engagements. In theory, these trips are seen as ways groups can get to know members, develop personal relationships, and ultimately influence members. The trips are considered fact-finding or offer groups ways to educate members by allowing them to collect information first hand. Although the ban was designed to stop improper uses of travel, the Jack Abramoff scandal is evidence of the potential problems of these trips. In an article by R. Jeffrey Smith and James Grimaldi (*Washington Post*, April 6, 2005) they described an instance where Tom DeLay (R-TX) traveled to Russia where he met business and government officials. Subsequent votes in the House were supportive of Russian business interests. The trip cost $57,238.00 and was supposedly properly funded, but it now appears that Abramoff helped arrange financial support for the trip. To measure trips we used the number of trips members took in their first two congresses. These data were reported in members' financial disclosure forms. Members who did not serve three terms were not included, since members file information on their fourth year in their fifth year. Thus, these members did not file disclosure forms for their fourth year. Finally, there were some members who had missing forms. Three of these members, Robert Scott (D-VA), Albert Wynn (D-MD), and J. C. Watts (R-OK), had only one missing year, and in this case we substituted the mean of the trips taken per year for the missing value. The forms for two members, Shelia Jackson-Lee (D-TX) and Martin Hoke (R-OH), were missing for more than one year, and these members were not included in the analysis. Again, we use OLS regression to control for several variables. Variables thought to affect the likelihood that interest groups would offer the member a trip and the likelihood that the member would take it were controlled for. We also controlled for members' income (see Chapter Two for discussion of its measure), age when they entered, and race (whites coded one and others coded zero). We also controlled for party, progressive ambition, and intra-institutional ambition (see Chapter Five for a discussion of these variables).[4]

To measure amount of honorarium members received from interest groups we use the total amount of money raised as honorarium. Members are no longer allowed to pocket this money but can donate honorarium to charity. These data, too, come from their financial disclosure forms.

Table 7.1. OLS Regression Comparing Citizen and Professional Legislators in PAC Money

| | % of receipts | | $ from PACs | |
	First Congress	Second Congress	First Congress	Second Congress
Progressive	-3.64	-.74	17.73	7.47
	(5.51)	(2.89)	(20.86)	(27.36)
Retrospective	3.61	-3.29*	-10.73	-25.71+
	(3.10)	(1.78)	(11.75)	(16.85)
Majority Party	12.17***	10.71***	56.55***	60.67***
	(3.42)	(1.81)	(12.93)	(17.11)
Party	5.48+	17.47***	41.57***	78.46***
	(3.36)	(2.89)	(12.73)	(27.32)
Party Unity	-.38**	-.25**	-2.16***	-2.85***
	(.18)	(.10)	(.69)	(.95)
Total Spent	-.025***	-.009***	.31***	.21***
	(.005)	(.002)	(.02)	(.02)
Percent Vote	-.28**	-.05	-1.80***	-2.35***
	(.14)	(.07)	(.54)	(.69)
103rd Congress	-25.81***	-3.57+	-74.04***	-93.61***
	(5.31)	(2.65)	(20.12)	(25.07)
104th Congress	-23.97***	-3.46	-79.32***	-54.88**
	(5.38)	(2.84)	(20.36)	(26.83)
105th Congress	-16.77***	.05	-13.72	-21.30
	(5.20)	(2.71)	(19.69)	(25.68)
Constant	125.52***	59.54***	396.28***	528.02***
	(21.34)	(10.57)	(80.82)	(99.97)
Adj. R^2	.16	.26	.75	.64
N	282	233	282	233

+< .20 * < .10 ** <.05 *** < .01 (using a two-tailed test)
Sources: *Almanac of American Politics*, (various years), *CQ's Biographies of Freshman Members* (various years), *CQ's Politics in America 2002*, *CQ's Weekly Reports* (various years), http://www.fec.gov, and http://opensecrets.org. Data calculated by authors. See Appendix A for explanation of the variables.

Findings

There is some but limited evidence to support the expectation that prospective citizen legislators will have less contact with interest groups.[5] According to Table 7.1, their PAC contributions were a slightly smaller percentage of reelection receipts but a slightly larger dollar figure. But none of the differences even neared statistical significance. Also these members were no more or less likely to become lobbyists when they leave (Table 7.2) or to go on fact-finding trips (Table 7.3). They did, however, accept fewer honorarium dollars. This difference neared statistical significance. With regard to retrospective citizen legislators they accepted less PAC money. They accepted significantly less PAC money in their second reelection bid, measured as both percentage and amount of money. In the first reelection bid the differences were not significant. Also there was no difference between whether they or other members became lobbyists. Finally, although they were more likely to go on fact-finding trips they accepted fewer honorariums. Again, neither of these differences were statistically significant.

The interviews with policy makers and the case studies support the above findings that there is little difference between citizen and professional legislators' relationships with interest groups. However, two citizen legislators believed they were driven by principle and thus not susceptible to interest group pressure. Former Rep. Tom Coburn (R-OK) indicated that he was not influenced by interest groups because he had his policy objectives in mind and was focused on principle, not his political career. Former member Rep. Mark Sanford (R-SC), in his book written during his time in office, also spoke of standing on principle and not being swayed by the attractions of life as a professional politician (Sanford 2000). Having principles driving members' decisions, however, does not necessarily mean that constituent's interests are represented since the principles may not aid constituents' interests. Also, principled members may have close relationships with groups who share their cause.

Another legislator also discussed value of interest groups. Former Rep. Tillie Fowler (R-FL), a prospective citizen legislator, said she was willing to meet with interest groups. Fowler recognized that sometimes interest groups had information that was not readily available. However, in her opinion this was just one step in the process of gathering information. She thought that solely relying on interest groups for information presented just a partial picture and that other viewpoints should be sought (Fowler 2004).

Additionally, Rep. Frank Lucas (R-OK), a professional legislator, noted that he did vote against the wishes of his voters in support of interest groups' positions. However, he believed that interest groups often do a poor job educating the voters and that by voting with the groups he actually was voting with the interests of the voters. He was, in essence, behaving as a trustee. Agricultural trade issues are very important to his constituents, and he lamented that farm groups "expect me to cast votes in a certain way because everyone knows it's in the best interests of the country and the corn growers, and the swine industry, for

Table 7.2. Logistic Regression Comparing Likelihood of Citizen and Professional Legislators Becoming Lobbyists

Prospective	-.01
	(.65)
Retrospective	.17
	(.48)
Party	-.94*
	(.49)
Age	-.04+
	(.03)
Year left	.08
	(.08)
Constant	-165.65
	(165.88)
Nagelkerke R^2	.12
Cox and Snell R^2	.08
N	105

+< .20 * < .10 ** <.05 *** < .01 (using a two-tailed test)

Sources: *Almanac of American Politics, CQ's Biographies of Freshman Members* (various years), *CQ's Politics in America 2002, CQ's Weekly Reports* (various years) and *Financial Disclosure Reports of House Members* (various congresses). Data calculated by authors.

See Appendix A for explanation of the variables.

Table 7.3. OLS Regression Comparing Citizen and Professional Legislators In Accepting Fact-finding Trips and Honoraria

	Fact-finding Trips	Honoraria
Prospective	-.08	-810.45+
	(1.96)	(513.40)
Retrospective	.77	-89.88
	(1.21)	(317.58)
Intra-institutional	5.41***	746.31+
	(1.80)	(472.21)
Progressive	.51	773.11*
	(1.76)	(460.83)
White	-8.43***	-1882.66
	(1.86)	(487.69)
Party	-.95	-397.44
	(1.29)	(338.67)
Age	-.14*	-29.12+
	(.08)	(19.95)
Income	.004+	.54
	(.003)	(.72)
103rd Congress	-2.92+	48.29
	(1.82)	(477.72)
104th Congress	1.98	-52.73
	(1.93)	(505.50)
105th Congress	1.00	700.14+
	(1.89)	(495.22)
Constant	19.92***	4191.31***
	(4.23)	(1160.93)
R^2	.17	.12
Adjusted R^2	.13	.08
N	224	224

$+ < .20$ $* < .10$ $** < .05$ $*** < .01$ (using a two-tailed test)

Sources: *Almanac of American Politics, CQ's Biographies of Freshman Members* (various years), *CQ's Politics in America 2002, CQ's Weekly Reports* (various years) and *Financial Disclosure Reports of House Members* (various congresses). Data calculated by authors.

See Appendix A for explanation of the variables.

example, but they fail to mention that to their rank and file membership back home" (Lucas 2004).

One staff member we interviewed who wished to remain anonymous believed newly arrived inexperienced members present a special dilemma for interest groups. But this dilemma did not mean that they ignored these members. In order to make their case, lobbyists have to take into account the members' background since some with a business background will have a much different take on an issue than a member with an academic background.

Conclusion

The evidence in this chapter suggests that there is a moderate difference with regard to citizen and professional legislators' contact with interest groups. The main difference we found was that retrospective citizen legislators raised less PAC money in their second reelection bid. We are confident that one of the reasons larger differences were not found was that political realities limit the effect that length of political career has on members' behavior. Regardless of length of political career, members know the value of interest groups in providing campaign resources and political information. Also, as noted earlier, the reason interest contact is valued may vary with the different types of members. Thus the difference could be more qualitative than quantitative.

Interest groups can take a short- and long-term approach to their interaction, monetary and non-monetary, with legislators. Even a legislator that is short-term will not be immune from interest group lobbying on a single must pass bill. The big difference is probably overall length of service, positions of authority, and whether the member is part of the majority party. In that instance, we would expect much more concerted efforts by interest groups to curry favor. Citizen and professional legislators with a short time of service are likely to be treated the same.

Notes

1. This is based on the question from the National Election Study, "Would you say the government is pretty much run by a few big interests looking out for themselves or that it is run for the benefit of all the people?"

2. Even though we do not look at members who have served a long time, one can make the argument that members who arrived on Capitol Hill with experience have already started to build relationships with certain interests and that interest groups may spend less time and energy cultivating relationships with members who have limited terms.

3. Although party and number of years in the majority party were highly correlated ($r=.80$, $p=.00$), we used them both in this equation since they both have significant independent relationships with the dependent variables.

4. We also considered controlling for gender, marital status, and being on a power committee, but these variables were so weakly related to number of trips members have taken that we did not include them in the analysis. Also, it should be noted in coding trips, no effort was made to separate trips paid for by interest groups, party organizations, or businesses, since each could concern a particular interest.

5. When all members who signed the pledge were considered to be prospective citizen legislators, the only significant difference was that its relationship with percent of receipts in the first reelection neared statistical significance (p.< .20). Appendix B suggest that the conclusions would be the same had the citizen legislator category excluded those exhibiting progressive ambition.

Chapter Eight
Conclusion

The low levels of trust in Congress and the nationwide push for term limits during the early 1990s spurred our interest in the possible impact that citizen legislators would have on the quality of representation in the House of Representatives. Our goal was an objective and empirical examination of whether citizen legislators differ from professional legislators in how they represent their constituents' interests. This was a difficult task. First, there was not a single accepted definition of a citizen legislator so we used two definitions of citizen legislator: one based on lacking a previous political career and the other on having limited future career (limited terms of service). Second, there are conflicting views of what is the best way to represent constituents' interests. Are the best representatives trustees or delegates? Do the best representatives work on the narrow interests of the district or the larger interests of the nation? Although there is no agreement as to the best style and focus of a representative, we focus primarily on representatives behaving as district-focused delegates. We believe this is most consistent with the structure of the U.S. House with its members serving relatively small districts and facing reelection every two years.

Third, the answers to two different debates shape people's views of the representational differences between citizen and professional legislators. The first debate concerns the relative values of private and political experiences. Citizen legislators may offer better representation than professional legislators because, having more experiences as private citizens, they better understand the needs of their constituents. Since they have more experience as private citizens, pursuing the type of life held by the majority of other citizens, they will understand the effects of laws and better know citizens' interests. Political experience too may be harmful. The power that comes with a political office is believed to corrupt individuals and distances them from the public, resulting in members focused on Washington and not their districts. Consequently, the less time and exposure members have to power and the perks of the office, the more likely they are to work on constituents' interests. On the other hand, some suggest that members' experience representing constituents is needed to understand the complex national issues and how to enact workable public policy. Political experience represents three things: an understanding of finer points of legislative procedure, constituents' interests, and the minutia of the issue. Private sphere influence too may increase the conflicts of interest and prevent detached debates. On that basis, professional politicians with their greater experience make the best representatives.

The second debate concerns the value of ambition and the resulting desire for reelection. On the one hand, citizen legislators are likely motivated to serve out of a different set of goals than professional legislators. They will work for constituents and not for themselves. Since citizen legislators are motivated by policy goals instead of career goals, they will act to advance good public policy without regard to the impact on their own careers. Citizen legislators, particularly prospective ones, may be better because they have less interest in reelection. This frees them from having to serve special interests, enabling them to focus on their districts' interests. On the other hand, reelection goals may encourage members to be responsive to their constituents and provide accountability, whereas citizen legislators who are presumably less interested in reelection are freer to go against the interests of their constituents and have less accountability. Ambition theory too suggests that members who are interested in political careers will guard their constituents' interests. They know all too well that their success in representing their constituents in the present will affect future reelection prospects.

On top of these debates, there are a host of other factors that affect members' legislative behavior. There are the requirements to hold office, such as political interest, knowledge, skills, and resources. There are the institutional practices, norms, and rules that can limit the effects of career length on members' behaviors. In addition, members in the minority party behave differently than those in the majority. This all leads us to be skeptical that great differences would be found between citizen and professional legislators, and we found few strong differences.

The expectation that citizen legislators make better representatives because they have similar experiences to their constituents leads to the presumption that descriptive representation is needed for substantive representation. However, we found few differences between citizen and professional legislators in their demographic characteristics. Both types of legislators were predominately more elite than the American population and their geographic constituency, and where there were differences, citizen legislators were generally more elite. That citizen legislators were not more "like" the people begs the question "why not?" We believe citizen legislators were not like the average American because of the institutional and non-institutional requirements it takes to be reelected. To run a successful campaign for Congress requires considerable time, money, and political connections, which are things most Americans lack. Even if average Americans have the resources to run a competitive campaign, it is unclear that the benefits of the office are great enough for most Americans. Life as a member of Congress involves living in a fish bowl, working long hours, spending time away from family, and sacrificing many other personal activities. Additionally, most voters prefer candidates who have qualities lacking in most Americans, such as political interest and skill.

The findings also beg the question, "If citizen legislators are not like the American people, are they still likely to have experiences similar to the people and better understand the people's needs?" The findings suggest that they are unlikely to have the experiences of blue collar workers, women, minorities, or the poor. Even if they grew up in poor or blue collar homes, their experiences are likely unique because they no longer possess those characteristics. This tends to limit their empathy and understanding of most Americans' lives.

Although citizen legislators are not likely to better understand the district's interests because they are more similar to their constituents than are professional legislators, they still could have a better understanding because they stay in better contact with their constituents. However, we found little difference between citizen and professional legislators in their levels of contact with constituents. Although none of the relationships were statistically significant, prospective citizen legislators consistently did less to stay in contact with their constituents than did prospective professional legislators while retrospective citizen legislator consistently did more to stay in contact. This indicates that while the weaker desire for a future in politics decreases the need to keep in contact, a lack of experience may slightly increase the members' felt need to maintain contact. Although our findings with regard to prospective citizen legislators were weak, they did support the conclusions of the effects of term limits at the state level. Carey, Niemi, and Powell (2000) found that term-limited state legislators were less likely to keep in contact with constituents than non-term-limited legislators. The analysis too implied that citizen legislators could have been going home as much for personal as political reasons. Lacking a political future with your constituents, we believe, weakens electoral concerns and the need members feel to keep in touch with their districts. In fact, the more electorally secure members were the less likely they were to keep in contact.

Although citizen legislators were not more likely to resemble their constituents or to keep in contact with them, they could still offer greater substantive representation if they represented districts that were likely to share their views. Two different analyses were conducted to see what differences, if any, existed between how citizen and professional legislators cast roll-call votes. First, we examined whether citizen or professional legislators were more ideological in their roll-call voting. If citizen legislators are motivated to pursue the adoption of certain policy goals, they may be less willing to compromise their principles and consequently appear more ideological. There was some evidence that citizen legislators were more ideological. Both prospective and retrospective citizen legislators had more extreme DW-NOMINATE scores than did professional legislators. Additionally, the more electorally secure members were, the more likely they were to have extreme voting records. The qualitative analysis implied that citizen legislators were less motivated to behave like delegates. They tended to say that they did what they felt was right or made decisions based on principles. There was some evidence too that retrospective citizen legislators voted more consistently with the ideological leanings of their districts. Thus, members who lack experience and ambition, and consequently are less focused on reelection, have more ideologically extreme voting records but only lack of experience has much effect on whether members' votes are consistent with the preferences of their constituents.

To represent constituents' interests, members also need to be effective policy makers. Citizen and professional legislators differ in how they achieve their policy goals. We concluded that prospective citizen legislators were slightly less active and effective than were others. Although prospective citizen legislators were generally similar to professional legislators with regard to levels of activity, they were less likely to cast votes. With regard to effectiveness, they were similar to others in media coverage and ability to pass amendments though they were significantly less likely to see the bills and resolutions they introduced pass, and be assigned to power committees. However, we do offer evidence that citizen legislators can be effective in other ways, particularly in blocking legislation they find undesirable. We do have suspicions, however, that the findings were affected by the narrow majority held by the Republicans. Retrospective citizen and professional legislators were similar in activity and effectiveness.

Good representatives should be ethical. Citizen legislators, contrary to popular belief, were more likely to have ethical conflicts than were professional legislators. This was true whether citizen legislators were defined as prospective or retrospective. Citizen legislators were more likely to have been accused of and found guilty of violating the House standards. There was also evidence from the qualitative analysis that citizen legislators have some of the same types of conflicts of interest as do professional legislators but additionally have some unique conflicts. This indicates that citizen legislators may be better able to work on their own behalf than on behalf of their constituents.

Finally, we examined differences between citizen and professional legislators with regard to their relationships with interest groups. It is feared that members who work too closely with interest groups work for these interests instead of those of their district. Generally, we conclude that prospective citizen legislators either had slightly weaker relationships with interest groups than did others or there was no difference. The only relationship that even neared statistical significance was that they accepted fewer honorarium dollars. Also, members who were running in closer elections accepted more PAC money, indicating that reelection concerns may increase members' willingness to take PAC dollars. Retrospective citizen legislators were also slightly less tied to interests groups than were others. They were less likely to take PAC money than were retrospective professional legislators, but otherwise were similar to them in their relationships to interests groups

The above discussion suggests that the way in which citizen legislators are defined affects the conclusions about differences between citizen and professional legislators. This is likely because the value of experience debate has more implications for retrospective citizen legislators and the ambition/reelection debate has more implications for prospective citizen legislators. On the one hand, the lack of ambition generally depressed members' interest in staying in contact with the district, while allowing for more extreme ideological voting. Likely this is because they have less interest in reelection. On the other hand, a lack of experience tended to slightly increase members' contact with the district, and vote with the districts' positions. This is likely because the inexperienced are less sure of how to act. Lacking experience and future ambition tended to moderate members' effectiveness. This trend was stronger for prospective citizen legislators than for retrospective citizen legislators. Prospective citizen legislators sometimes had more contact and sometimes had less contact with interest groups, while retrospective citizen legislators had fewer PAC contributions, at least in the second reelection bid. However, most of these findings were fairly weak indicating that more than the type of experience a member had or the future ambition a member has affects his or her behavior.

The Role of Elections and Ambition

One of the key explanations for why citizen and professional legislators should differ rests with elections. On the one hand, citizen legislators may be less concerned or focused on elections. Consequently, they should be better able to devote time and energy on their policy objectives and be less connected to interest groups. On the other hand, this freedom from the constraining effects of elections may make members less accountable and thus poorer representatives. In many of our analyses we controlled for the closeness of elections. If the desire for reelection affects members' behavior we would expect, all things being equal, these effects should be most pronounced for those running in marginal districts, i.e., districts likely to swing to the other party. We found that members running in marginal districts behaved in ways that signify their strong desire to win the support of their district. The more marginal members' districts are, the more PAC money they raise, the more travel they make to the district, and the more staff they put in the district. They were also less ideological and less likely to support the party; presumably to gain votes, they were willing to go to the middle of the political spectrum and go against the party. We also found evidence that they were effective members, likely to be assigned to a power committee and a conference committee, and likely to see their amendments pass. They were also more active proposing amendments but cast fewer roll-call votes. These findings are consistent with the theories that suggest elections connect members to their districts and mold their behavior. Members running in marginal districts behaved more like district-focused delegates than did other members.

The above suggests that if reformers want to insure that members are responsive and accountable to the voters the key is not members' career goals but competitive elections. It is competitive elections that keep members legislatively active and effective. Granted, term limits could have the effect of increasing electoral competition by deleting the incumbency advantage.

However, research has not been conclusive as to that effect (see Farmer et al. 2003 for examples).

Our findings also support ambition theory. Members with intra-institutional ambition demonstrated their understanding of power in the processes. They were more likely to go on junkets, accepted more honoraria, more likely to see the amendments they introduced pass, and received more media coverage. These are all activities likely to help them demonstrate their leadership abilities to other members in order to win leadership posts. Members with progressive ambition also behaved in ways likely to build support in their districts such as making more trips to the district; and having less staff in the district, presumably to have D.C. staff to work on issues of interest to a larger constituency. They also accepted more honoraria. It may be that giving talks increased their visibility and the honorarium can be given to organization that can help with future elections. This, too, supports the idea that reelection goals keep members close to their constituents. Members who want to get reelected or want to be elected by a larger constituency will behave in ways to keep in touch and represent constituent wishes.

Based on the evidence that electoral factors and political ambition affect members' behavior in predicted ways, it is on the surface surprising that our citizen legislators did not differ more from professional legislators. We believe this is because although our citizen legislators may have had different career lengths, particularly future career, they still had enough interest in reelection to work toward that end. They would not have sought and won a House seat if they were average in their political ambition or skills. It is not that citizen legislators lack political ambition and a desire for reelection, it is only that they have less ambition and desire for reelection.

Appendix A: Description of Variable Codes and Data Sources

Variable names are in bold and listed in alphabetical order.

% of Receipts—percent of campaign donations from PACs. Data come from *OpenSecrets* (opensecrets.org) and the Federal Elections Commission (http://www.fec.gov).

% Staff in District—mean percent of staff in district offices. Based on data from the *Congressional Directory*, various years.

$ from PACs—amount of money contributed by PACs. Data come from *Open-Secrets* (opensecrets.org) and the Federal Elections Commission (http://www. fec.gov).

$ Spent on Franking—mean amount of money spent on franking in first two congresses. This data comes from the Clerk of the House's report on disbursements.

103rd Congress—first congress entered.

1	Yes
0	No

104th Congress—first congress entered.

1	Yes
0	No

105th Congress—first congress entered.

1	Yes
0	No

Age—age when member entered the House. Based on information from CQ's freshmen biographies.

Amendments—mean number of amendments introduced by member in first two congresses. Data from *Thomas* website (thomas.loc.gov).

Amendments Passed—did member have one amendment pass during first two congresses? Data from *Thomas* website (thomas.loc.gov).

1	Yes
0	No

Bills and Resolutions—mean number of bills and resolutions introduced by member in first two congresses. Data from *Thomas* website (thomas.loc.gov).

Bills and Resolutions Passed—did member have one bill or resolution pass during first two congresses? Data from *Thomas* website (thomas.loc.gov).

1	Yes
0	No

Conference Committee—was member appointed to a conference committee?

       1   Yes

       0   No

Difference Age—difference between member's age and median district age.

Difference College—difference between whether a member had a college degree (coded 1) and percent of member's district with a college degree.

Difference Income—difference between member's income and median income in the district.

Difference Gender—difference between whether a member was female (coded 1) and percent of member's district that was female.

Difference Race—difference between whether a member was white (coded 1) and percent of member's district that was white.

Difference Party—difference between whether member party (coded 1) and percent of member's district with voting for that party in presidential races.

District Age—median age for the district. Data from the *Congressional Districts in the 1990s*.

District Education—percentage of district population with a college degree. Data from the *Congressional Districts in the 1990s*.

District Race—percentage of the district population that not white. Data from the *Congressional Districts in the 1990s*.

District Republican—mean percentage of vote going to Republican presidential candidate, 1992, 1996, 2000. Data from *CQs Politics in America* (various years).

DW-NOMINATE—scores range from 1 for conservative roll-call voting to -1 for liberal role-call voting. These are based on the first dimension. Data come from http://voteview.com/dwnomin.htm.

Education—*Congressional Quarterly* biographies of freshmen members of Congress.

       1   Less than high school education

       2   High school diploma

       3   College degree

       4   Graduate education

Electoral Security—Mean percentage of the district's two-party vote going to the president's party, 1992, 1996, and 2000. Data from *CQ's Politics in America* (various years).

Fact-finding Trips—number of fact-finding trips (junkets) taken by members. Data come from financial disclosure forms.

Gender—member's gender.

       1   Female

       0   Male

Income—calculated from member's financial disclosure statements submitted to Congress. The figures represent are standardized in 1999 dollars.

Intra-institutional—member considered to have intra-institutional ambition if he/she sought leadership position in House.

       1   Intra-institutional Ambition

       0   No intra-institutional Ambition

Judiciary Committee—was member on Judiciary Committee when Pres. Clinton was impeached?

    1   Yes

    0   No

Lawyers—whether member is a lawyer.

    1   Lawyer

    0   Not a lawyer

Lobbyist—did member become lobbyist after leaving Congress? Data from Clerk of the House list of registered lobbyists.

    1   Yes

    0   No

Majority Party—whether member is part of majority party.

    0   None

    1   1 of first two congresses

    2   First two congresses

Media Coverage—mean number of stories in the *Washington Post* that mention the member by name for his/her first two congresses.

Party—member's party affiliation.

    1   Democratic Party

    0   Republican Party

Party Strength—mean percentage of the district's two-party vote going to the president's party, 1992, 1996, and 2000. Data from *CQ's Politics in America* (various years).

Party Unity—mean party unity scores for first two congresses, corrected for non-attendance. Taken from *CQ Weekly Reports* (various years).

Percent Vote—percent vote for member in election. Data come from *CQ Weekly Reports* (various years).

Power Committee—was member appointed to a power committee (Budget, Appropriations, Ways and Means, and Rules)?

    1   Yes

    0   No

Progressive Ambition—member considered progressive if he/she sought higher office.

    1   Progressive Ambition

    0   Not Progressive Ambition

Prospective Citizen Legislator—did member sign and keep the term limits pledge?

    1   Yes

    0   No

Race (white) —member's race.

    1   White

    0   Non-white

Retrospective Citizen Legislator—does member have significant prior political experience?

> 1   No experience
> 0   Experienced

Total Spent—amount spent by member in election. Data come from the Federal Elections Committee (www.fec.gov).

Travel—mean amount of money spent on travel back to district by member and staff for first two congresses. This data comes from the Clerk of the House's report on disbursements.

Virginia/Maryland—does member live in Virginia or Maryland?

> 1   Yes
> 0   No

Voting Participation—mean percent of time member cast votes on roll-call votes for first two congresses. Data come from *CQ Congressional Almanac* (various years) and *CQ Weekly Reports* (various years).

Appendix B: Difference of Means for Term-Limited Members With and Without Progressive Ambition

Dependent Variable	Non-progressive Ambition	Progressive Ambition	Probability
Chapter Two			
Members' characteristics:			
Education	3.50	3.64	.52
Income	287.45	192.47	.42
White	1.00	1.00	
Female	.21	.00	.07
Age	49.14	40.86	.02
Lawyer	.21	.36	.42
Party	.21	.07	.30
Compared to district:			
Education	.75	.83	.11
Income	241.80	143.91	.35
White	.09	.12	.17
Female	.51	.52	.01
Age	14.64	7.75	.06
Party	.53	.55	.29
Chapter Three			
Travel	29887.57	29881.88	.999
% Staff	.21	.14	.35
$ Spent on Frank	44809.52	35441.71	.40
Chapter Four			
DW-NOMINATE	..35	.46	.42
DW-NOMINATE(Abs)	.49	.51	.76
Party Unity	87.64	92.31	.19
Chapter Five			
Bills and Resolutions	9.46	9.21	.90
Amendments	2.79	1.21	.02
Voting Participation	97.25	96.86	.61
Bills Passed	.43	.64	.27
Amendments Passed	.86	.79	.64
Media Coverage	14.07	16.25	.67
Conference	.64	.57	.71
Power Committee	.14	.21	.64

Appendix B

Dependent Variable	Non-progressive Ambition	Progressive Ambition	Probability
Chapter Six			
Accused	.14	.07	.56
Convicted	.07	.00	.33
Chapter Seven			
% PAC first	37.98	28.26	.16
$ PAC first	327.14	267.36	.50
% PAC second	37.03	30.99	.43
$ PAC second	332.71	234.79	.32
Fact-finding Trips	5.31	10.15	.42
Honorarium	600.00	867.31	.65

Appendix C: Ethics Rules

House Rule XLIII: Code of Official Conduct

1. A member, officer, or employee of the House of Representatives shall conduct himself at all times in a manner that shall reflect creditably on the House of Representatives.

2. A Member, officer, or employee of the House of Representatives shall adhere to the spirit and the letter of the Rules of the House of Representatives and to the rules of duly constituted committees thereof.

3. A Member, officer, or employee of the House of Representatives shall receive no compensation nor shall he permit any compensation to accrue to his beneficial interest from any source, the receipt of which would occur by virtue of influence improperly exerted from his position in Congress.

4. A Member, officer, or employee of the House of Representatives shall not accept gifts (other than personal hospitality of an individual or with a fair market value of $100 or less) in any calendar year aggregation more than $250, directly or indirectly, from any person (other than from a relative) except to the extent permitted by written waiver granted in exceptional circumstances by the Committee on Standards of Official Conduct pursuant to clause 4(e) (1) (E) of rule X.

5. A Member, officer, or employee of the House of Representatives, shall accept no honorarium for a speech, writing for publication, or other similar activity.

6. A Member of the House of Representatives shall keep his campaign funds separate from his personal funds. A Member shall convert no campaign funds to personal use in excess of reimbursement for legitimate and verifiable campaign expenditures and shall expend no funds from his campaign account not attributable to bona fide campaign or political purposes.

7. A Member of the House of Representatives shall treat as campaign contributions all proceeds from testimonial dinners or other fund raising events.

8. A Member or officer of the House of Representatives shall retain no one under his payroll authority who does not perform official duties commensurate with the compensation received in the offices of the employing authority. In the case of committee employees who work under the direct supervision of a Member other than a chairman, the chairman may require that such Member affirm in writing that the employees have complied with the preceding sentence (subject to clause 6 of rule XI) as evidence of the chairman's compliance with this clause and with clause 6 of rule XI.

9. A Member, officer, or employee of the House of Representatives shall not discharge or refuse to hire any individual, or otherwise discriminate against any individual with respect to compensation, terms, conditions, or privileges or employment, because of such individual's race, color, religion, sex (including marital or parental status), age, or national origin, but may take into consideration the domicile or political affiliation of such individual.

10. A Member of the House of Representatives who has been convicted by a court of record for the commission of a crime for which a sentence of two or more years imprisonment may be imposed should refrain from participation in the business of each com-

mittee of which he is a member and should refrain from voting on any question at a meeting of the House, or of the Committee of the Whole House, unless or until judicial or executive proceedings result in reinstatement of the presumption of his innocence or until he is reelected to the House after the date of such conviction.

11. A Member of the House of Representatives shall not authorize or otherwise allow a non-House individual, group, or organization to use the words "Congress of the United States", "House of Representatives", or "Official Business", or any combination of words thereof, on any letterhead or envelope.

12. (a) Except as provided by paragraph (b), any employee of the House of Representatives who is required to file a report pursuant to rule XLIV shall refrain from participating personally and substantially as an employee of the House of Representatives in any contact with any agency of the executive or judicial branch of Government with respect to nonlegislative matters affecting any nongovernmental person in which the employee has a significant financial interest.

(b) Paragraph (a) shall not apply if an employee first advises his employing authority of his significant financial interest and obtains from his employing authority a written waiver stating that the participation of the employee is necessary. A copy of each such waiver shall be filed with the Committee on Standards of Official Conduct.

Source: http://www.house.gov/ethics

References

Aldrich, J. H., and D. W. Rohde. 2000. The Consequences of Party Organization in the House: The Role of Majority and Minority Parties in Conditional Party Government. In *Polarized Politics: Congress and the President in a Partisan Era*, edited by J. R. Bond, and R. Fleisher, 31-72. Washington, D.C.: CQ Press.

Aldrich, J. H., and D. W. Rohde. 2001. The Logic of Conditional Party Government: Revisiting the Electoral Connection. In *Congress Reconsidered,* seventh ed., edited by L. C. Dodd, and B. I. Oppenheimer, 269-92. Washington, D.C.: CQ Press.

Allen, T. 2004. Telephone interview with S. H. Fisher III.

Allenbaugh, X., and N. Pinney. 2003. The Real Costs of Term Limits: Comparative Study of Competition and Electoral Costs. In *Test of Time: Coping with Legislative Term Limits*, edited by R. Farmer, D. J. Rausch, and J. C. Green, 161-76. New York: Lexington Books.

Andersen, K. 1997. Gender and Public Opinion. In *Understanding Public Opinion*, edited by B. Norrander and C. Wilcox, 19-36. Washington D.C.: CQ Press.

Anonymous. 2004. Interview with S. H. Fisher III.

Armor, J. C. 1994. *Why Term Limits? Because They Have It Coming!* Ottawa, IL: Jameson Books, Inc.

Aved, R., Levy, D., and Tien, C. 2001. Do Differences Matter: The Impact of Women in Congress. *Women and Politics* 23: 105-27.

Bardes, B. A., and R. W. Oldendick. 2003. *Public Opinion: Measuring the American Mind*, second ed. Belmont, CA: Thomas Wadsworth.

Barone, M., and G. Ujifusa. 1993. *The Almanac of American Politics 1994.* Washington, D.C.: National Journal.

Barone, M., and G. Ujifusa. 1995. *The Almanac of American Politics 1996.* Washington, D.C.: National Journal.

Berkman, M. B. 1993. Former State Legislators in the U.S. House of Representatives: Institutional and Policy Mastery. *Legislative Studies Quarterly* 18: 77-104.

Bernstein, R. A. 1989. *Elections, Representation, and Congressional Voting Behavior: The Myth of Constituency Control*. Englewood Cliffs, NJ: Prentice-Hall, Inc.

Bickers, K. N., and R. M. Stein. 1996. The Electoral Dynamics of the Federal Pork Barrel. *American Journal of Political Science* 40: 1300-26.

Bingham, C. 1997. *Women on the Hill: Challenging the Culture of Congress.*

New York: Random House Times Books.

Bond, J. R. and R. Fleisher. 2000. *Polarized Politics: Congress and the President in a Partisan Era.* Washington, D.C.: CQ Press.

Boulard, G. 1994. Basic Training for Congress. *State Legislatures* July: 51-55.

Brainerd, K. 1999. Several Term Limits Supporters Recant Vows to Leave House, Saying Their Work Is Not Yet Done. *CQ Weekly*: 1444.

Browning, R. P., and H. Jacob. 1964. Power Motivation and the Political Personality. *Public Opinion Quarterly* 28: 75-90.

Cain, B. 1994. Term Limits: Not the Answer to What Ails Politics. In *The Politics and Law of Term Limits*, edited by E. H. Crane, and R. Pilon, 27-43. Washington, D.C.: Cato Institute.

Campbell, A., P. E. Converse, W. E. Miller, and D. E. Stokes. 1960. *The American Voter.* New York: Wiley.

Canon, D. T. 1999. *Race, Redistricting, and Representation: The Unintended Consequences of Black Majority Districts.* Chicago, IL: University of Chicago Press.

Carey, J. M. 1994. Political Shirking and the Last Term Problem: Evidence for a Party-Administered Pension System. *Public Choice* 81: 1-22.

Carey, J. M., R. G. Niemi, and L. W. Powell. 2000. *Term Limits: In the State Legislatures.* Ann Arbor, MI: University of Michigan Press.

Caro, R. A. 1981. *The Years of Lyndon Johnson: The Path to Power.* New York: Vintage Books.

Carroll, S. J. 1989. The Personal is Political: The Intersection of Private Lives and Public Roles among Women and Men in Elective and Appointive Office. *Women and Politics* 9: 51-67.

Carroll, S. J., and K. Jenkins. 2001. Unrealized Opportunity? Term Limits and the Representation of Women in State Legislatures. *Women and Politics* 23: 1-30.

Church, E. 1999. Agriculture Spending Bill Grinds to a Halt Under A Bushel of Amendments. *Congressional Quarterly Weekly Reports*: 1271-72.

Coburn, T. 2003. *Breach of Trust: How Washington Turns Outsiders into Insiders.* Nashville, TN: WND Books.

Congressional Staff Directory (various years). Washington, D.C.: CQ Press.

Congressional Districts in the 1990s: A Portrait of America. 1993 Washington, DC: Congressional Quarterly Press.

Congressional Record. 1995. *Debates on Term Limits Legislation.* Washington, D.C.

Constantini, E. 1990. Political Women and Political Ambition: Closing the Gender Gap. *American Journal of Political Science* 34: 741-70.

Constantini, E., and L. O. Valenty. 1996. The Motives-Ideology Connection among Political Party Activists. *Political Psychology* 17: 497-524.

Conway, M. M. 1991. *Political Participation in the United States*, second ed. Washington, D.C.: CQ Press.

Conway, M. M., G. A. Steuernagel, and D. W. Ahern. 1997. *Women and Political Participation.* Washington, D.C.: CQ Press.

Darcy, R., Welch, S., and J. Clark. 1994. *Women, Elections, and Representation*, second ed. Lincoln, NE: University of Nebraska Press.

Deering, C. J., and S. S. Smith. 1997. *Committees in Congress*, third ed. Washington, D.C.: CQ Press.

Delli Carpini, M. X. 1986. *Stability and Change in American Politics: The Coming of Age of the Generation of the 1960s*. New York: New York University Press.

Dodson, D. L. 1997. Change and Continuity in the Relationship between Private Responsibilities and Public Officeholding: The More Things Change, the More They Stay the Same. *Policy Studies* 25: 569-84.

Dolan, J. 1997. Support for Women's Interests in the 103rd Congress: The Distinct Impact of Congressional Women. *Women and Politics* 18: 81-94.

Emig, A. G., M. B. Hesse, and S. H. Fisher III. 1996. Black-White Differences in Political Efficacy. *Urban Affairs Review* 32: 264-76.

Erikson, R. S. and K. L. Tedin. 2001. *American Public Opinion*, sixth ed. New York: Longman Publishers.

Evans, D. 1996. Before the Roll-Call: Interest Group Lobbying and Public Policy Outcomes in House Committees. *Political Research Quarterly* 49: 287-304.

Farmer, R, J. D. Rausch Jr., and J. C. Green. 2003. *The Test of Time: Coping with Legislative Term Limits*. New York: Lexington Books.

Fenno, R. F., Jr. 1977. U.S. House Members in Their Constituencies: An Exploration. *American Political Science Review* 71: 883-917.

Fiorina, M. 1989. *Congress—Keystone of the Washington Establishment*, second ed. New Haven, CT: Yale University Press.

Fishel, J. 1971. Ambition and the Political Vocation: Congressional Challengers in American Politics. *Journal of Politics* 33: 25-56.

Foerstel, K., and H. Foerstel. 1996. *Climbing the Hill: Gender Conflict in Congress*. Westport, CT: Praeger.

Follman, M. 2003. Filler'up up—with taxpayer dollars. http://archive.salon.com /news/feature/2003/12/12/waxman/index.html.

Fowler, L. L. 1992. A Comment on Competition and Careers. In *Limiting Legislative Terms*, edited by G. Benjamin, and M. J. Malbin, 181-85. Washington, D.C.: CQ Press.

Fowler, T. 2004. Telephone interview with S. H. Fisher III.

Fox, R. L. and J. L. Lawless. 2004. Entering the Arena? Gender and the Decision to Run for Office. *American Journal of Political Science* 48: 264-80.

Frantzich, S. 1979. Who Makes Our Laws? The Legislative Effectiveness of Members of the U.S. House of Representatives. *Legislative Studies Quarterly* 4: 409-28.

Fried, A. 1997. *Muffled Echoes*. New York: Columbia University Press.

Fund, J. 1992. Term Limitation: An Idea Whose Time Has Come. In *Limiting Legislative Terms*, edited by G. Benjamin, and M. J. Malbin. Washington, D.C.: CQ Press.

Gartzke, E. and J. M. Wrighton. 1998. Thinking Globally or Acting Locally?

Determinants of the GATT Vote in Congress. *Legislative Studies Quarterly* 23: 33-55.

Gay, C. 2002. Spirals of Trust? The Effect of Descriptive Representation on the Relationship Between Citizens and Their Government. *American Journal of Political Science* 46: 717-32.

Gertzog, I. N. 1995. *Congressional Women: Their Recruitment, Integration, and Behavior*, second ed. Westport, CT: Praeger.

Giroux, G., S. Dougherty, K. Foerstel, and D. Willis. 2000. 21 GOP-Held House Seats Up for Grabs in November As Retirement List Grows. *CQ Weekly*: 56-57.

Greenblatt, A. 1997. House Passes Agriculture Bill After Coburn Gets $103 Million Cut. *Congressional Quarterly Weekly Report*: 1374-76.

Grenzke, J. M. 1989. PACs and the Congressional Supermarket: The Currency is Complex. *American Journal of Political Science* 33: 1-24.

Haider-Markel, D. 1999. Redistributing Values in Congress: Interest Group Influence Under Sub-optimal Conditions. *Political Research Quarterly* 52: 113-45.

Hall, R. L., and F. W. Wayman. 1990. Buying Time: Moneyed Interests and the Mobilization of Bias in Congressional Committees. *American Political Science Review* 84: 797-820.

Hamilton, A., J. Madison, and J. Jay. 1976. *The Federalist*. Washington, D.C.: Robert B. Luce, Inc.

The Hastings Center. 1985. *The Ethics of Legislative Life*. New York: The Hastings Center.

Hero, R. E. and C. J. Tolbert. 1995. Latinos and Substantive Representation in the U.S. House of Representatives: Direct, Indirect, or Nonexistent?" *American Journal of Political Science* 39: 640-52.

Herrera, C. L., R. Herrera, and E. R. N. Smith. 1992. Public Opinion and Congressional Representation. *Public Opinion Quarterly* 56: 185-205.

Herrick, R. 2003. *Fashioning the More Ethical House of Representatives: The Impact of Ethics Reforms in the U.S. House of Representatives*. New Haven, CT: Praeger.

———. 2004. Gender Differences in Early Congressional Retirement. *Politics and Policy* 32: 397-411.

Herrick, R., and M. K. Moore. 1993. Political Ambition's Effect on Legislative Behavior. *Journal of Politics* 55: 765-76.

Herrick, R., M. K. Moore, and J. R. Hibbing. 1994. Unfastening the Electoral Connection: The Behavior of U.S. Representatives When Reelection is No Longer a Factor. *Journal of Politics* 56: 214-27.

Herrick, R., and S. Thomas. 2005. Do Term Limits Make a Difference? Ambition and Motivations among U.S. State Legislators. *American Politics Research* 33: 726-47.

Hershey, M. R., and P. A. Beck. 2003. *Party Politics in America*, tenth ed. New York: Longman Publishers.

Heywood, P. 1997. Political Corruption: Problems and Perspectives. *Political Studies* 45: 417-36.

Hibbing, J. R. 1984. The Liberal Hour: Electoral Pressures and Transfer Payment Voting in the United States Congress. *The Journal of Politics* 46: 846-65.

———. 1991. Contours of the Modern Congressional Career. *American Political Science Review* 85: 405-28.

Hibbing, J. R., and E. Theiss-Morse. 1995. *Congress as Public Enemy*. Cambridge: Cambridge University Press.

Hibbing, J. R., and S. Thomas. 1990. The Modern United States Senate: What is Accorded Respect. *Journal of Politics* 42: 126-45.

Holian, D. B., Krebs, T. B., and Walsh, M. H. 1997. Constituency Opinion, Ross Perot, and Roll-Call Behavior in the U.S. House: The Case of NAFTA. *Legislative Studies Quarterly* 23: 369-92.

Huckabee, D. C. 2002. Length of Congressional Service: First Through 107th Congresses. *CRS Report for Congress*.

Huddy, L. and H. Terkildsen. 1993. The Consequences of Gender Stereotypes for Women Candidates at Different Levels and Types of Office. *Political research Quarterly* 46: 503-25.

Jacob, P. 1994. From the Voters with Care. In *The Politics and Law of Term Limits*, edited by E. H. Crane, and R. Pilon, 27-43. Washington, D.C.: Cato Institute.

Jacobson, G. C. 1987. Running Scared: Elections and Congressional Politics in the 1980s. In *Congress: Structure and Policy*, edited by M. D. McCubbins and T. Sullivan, 39-81. New York: Cambridge University Press.

Jeydel, A. and A. J. Taylor. 2003. Are Women Legislators Less Effective? Evidence for the U.S. House in the 103rd-105th Congress. *Political Research Quarterly* 56: 19-27.

Jennings, M. K., and R. G. Niemi. 1974. *The Political Character of Adolescence: The Influence of Families and Schools*. Princeton, NJ: Princeton University Press.

Kathlene, L. 1995. Alternative Views of Crime: Legislative Policymaking in Gendered Terms. *Journal of Politics* 57: 696-723.

Katz, J. 1997. Stance on Education Programs Set Up Battle Over Labor Bill. *Congressional Quarterly Weekly Report*: 2150-53.

Katz, J., and L. Nitschke. 1997. Fetal Tissue Study to Union Vote: Issues Delay Labor-HHS Bill. *Congressional Quarterly Weekly Report*: 2083-86.

Kerr, B. and W. Miller. 1997. Latino Representation, It's Direct and Indirect. *American Journal of Political Science* 41: 1066-71.

Kertzer, D. I. 1983. Generations as a Sociological Problem. *Annual Review of Sociology* 9: 125-49.

Kinder, D. R., M. D. Peters, R. P. Abeelson, and S. T. Fiske. 1980. Presidential Prototypes. *Political Behavior* 2: 315-37.

Kingdon, J. W. 1989. *Congressmen's Voting Decisions*, second ed. New York: Harper and Row, Publishers, Inc.

Kornberg, A., and N. Thomas. 1965. The Political Socialization of National Legislative Elites in the United States and Canada. *Journal of Politics* 27: 761-75.

Koszczuk, J. 1997. Gingrich's Friends Turn to Foes As Frustration Builds. *Congressional Quarterly Weekly Report*: 679-81.

Kuklinski, J. H. 1978. Representativeness and Elections: A Policy Analysis. *American Political Science Review* 72: 165-77.

Laswell, H. D. 1974. The Political Personality. In *Personality and Politics*, edited by G. J. DeRenzo. New York: Anchor Books.

Lawless, J. 2004. Politics of Presence? Congresswomen and Symbolic Representation. *Political Research Quarterly* 55: 81-99.

Little, T. H., and M. K. Moore. 1996. Been There, Done That, But Did It Matter? Former State Legislators in Congress. *Congress and the Presidency* 23: 103-12.

Lott, J. R., Jr. 1990. Attendance Rates, Political Shirking, and the Effects of Post-Elective Office Employment. *Economic Inquiry* 28: 133-50.

Louison, D. 1988. State Legislatures: The Proving Ground for National Leadership. *State Legislatures* July, 41-44.

Lucas, F. 2004. Telephone interview with S. H. Fisher III.

Madison, J. 2001a. Federalist Paper 56. In *The Federalists*, edited by G. Carey, and J. McClellan. Indianapolis, IN: Liberty Fund.

———. 2001b. Federalist Paper 57. In *The Federalists*, edited by G. Carey, and J. McClellan. Indianapolis, IN: Liberty Fund.

Malbin, M. J. 1992. Federalists v. Antifederalists: The Term-Limitation Debate at the Founding. In *Limiting Legislative Term*, edited by G. Benjamin and M. J. Malbin, 53-62. Washington, D.C.: CQ Press.

Mansbridge, J. 1999. Should Blacks Represent Blacks and Women Represent Women? A Contingent Yes. *Journal of Politics* 61: 628-57.

———. Rethinking Representation. *American Political Science Review* 97: 515-28.

Marinez, G. 1999. The Coburn Effect. *CQ Weekly* 57: 1355.

Mayhew, D. R. 1974. *Congress: The Electoral Connection*. New Haven, Connecticut: Yale University Press.

Miller, A. H., M. P. Wattenberg, and O. Malanchuk. 1986. Schematic Assessments of Presidential Candidates. *American Political Science Review* 80: 521-40

Miller, W. E., and Stokes, D. E. 1963. Constituency Influence in Congress. *American Political Science Review* 57: 45-56.

Niemi, R. G. and L. Powell. 2003. Limited Citizenship? Knowing and Contacting State Legislators after Term Limits. In *The Test of Time: Coping with Legislative Term Limits*, edited by R. Farmer, J. D. Rausch, and J. C. Green, 193-209. New York: Lexington Books.

Olson, D. M., and C. Nonidez. 1972. Measures of Legislative Performance in the U.S. House of Representatives. *Midwest Journal of Political Science* 16: 269-77.

Ornstein, N., T. E. Mann, and M. J. Malbin. 2002. *Vital Statistics on Congress: 2001-2002*. Washington, D.C.: American Enterprise Institute.

Ota, A. 1998. Road Wars and Special Projects Ensure House Bill's Rough Ride. *Congressional Quarterly Weekly Reports*: 809-11.

Payne, J. L. 1984. *The Motivation of Politicians*. Chicago, IL: Nelson-Hall Publishers.

Peaden, C., and R. Herrick. 2001. Citizen Coburn: A Study of Rotation in Office. Stillwater, OK.

Petracca, M. P. 1992. Rotation in Office: The History of an Idea. In *Limiting Legislative Terms*, edited by G. Benjamin, and M. J. Malbin, 19-52. Washington, D.C.: CQ Press.

Pitkin, H. 1967. *The Concept of Representation*. Berkeley, CA: University of California Press.

Reingold, B. 2000. *Representing Women: Sex, Gender, and Legislative Behavior in Arizona and California*. Chapel Hill, NC: University of North Carolina Press.

Rosenstone, S. J., and J. M. Hansen. 1993. *Mobilization, Participation, and Democracy in America*. New York: McMillan Publishing Company.

Rosenthal, A. 1996. *Drawing the Line: Legislative Ethics in the States*. Lincoln, NE: University of Nebraska Press.

Rothenberg, L. S., and M. S. Sanders. 2000. Severing the Electoral Connection: Shirking the Contemporary Congress. *American Journal of Political Science* 44: 316-25.

Sanford, M. 2000. *The Trust Committed to Me*. Washington, D.C.: U.S. Term Limits Foundation.

Schlesinger, J. A. 1966. *Ambition and Politics*. Chicago, IL: Rand McNally.

Shepsle, K. A., and B. R. Weingast. 1987. The Institutional Foundations of Committee Power. *American Political Science Review* 81: 85-104.

Stewart C. III. 1994. Let's Go Fly a Kite: Correlates of Involvement in the House Bank Scandel. *Legislative Studies Quarterly* 19: 521-35.

Swain, C. M. 1993. *Black Faces, Black Interests: The Representation of African Americans in Congress*. Cambridge, MA: Harvard University Press.

Swers, M. L. 2002. Transforming the Agenda: Analyzing Gender Differences in Women's Issue Bill Sponsorship. In *Women Transforming Congress*, edited by C. S. Rosenthal, 260-83. Norman, OK: Oklahoma University Press.

Swers, M. 2001. Understanding the Policy Impact of Electing Women: Evidence from Research on Congress and State Legislatures. *PS: Political Science and Politics* 34: 217-20.

Tate, K. 2001. The Political Representation of Blacks in Congress: Does Race Matter? *Legislative Studies Quarterly* 25: 623-38.

———. 2003. *Black Faces in the Mirror: African Americans and Their Representatives in the U.S. Congress*. Princeton, NJ: Princeton University Press.

Thomas, S. 1994. *How Women Legislate*. New York: Oxford Press.

Thomas, S., R. Herrick, and M. Braunstein. 2003. Legislative Careers: The Personal and Political. In *Women Transforming Congress*, edited by C. S.

Rosenthal, 397-421. Norman, OK: Oklahoma University Press.

Thompson, D. F. 1995. *Ethics in Congress: From Individual to Institutional Corruption*. Washington, D.C.: The Brookings Institution.

Tyler, T. R. 1990. *Why People Obey the Law*. New Haven, CT: Yale University Press.

U.S. Term Limits, Inc. v. Thornton. 1995 115 S.Ct. 1842.

Van Der Silk, J. R., and S. I. Pernacciaro. 1979. Office Ambitions and Voting Behavior in the U.S. Senate: A Longitudinal Study. *American Politics Quarterly* 7: 198-224.

Vega, A., and J. M. Firestone. 1995. The Effects of Gender on Congressional Behavior and Substantive Representation of Women. *Legislative Studies Quarterly* 20: 213-22.

Walsh, K. C. 2002. Enlarging Representation: Women Bringing Marginalized Perspectives to Floor Debate in the House of Representatives. In *Women Transforming Congress*, edited by C. S. Rosenthal, 370-96. Norman, OK: Oklahoma University Press.

Weisberg, H. F., E. S. Heberling, and L. M. Campoli, eds. 1999. *Classics in Congressional Politics*. New York: Longman.

Will, G. F. 1993. *Restoration: Congress, Term Limits and the Recovery of Deliberative Democracy*. New York: Free Press.

Wolbrecht, C. 2002. Female Legislators and the Women's Rights Agenda: From Feminine Mystique to Feminist Era. In *Women Transforming Congress*, edited by C. S. Rosenthal, 170-239. Norman, OK: Oklahoma University Press.

Wright, G. 2004. Do Term Limits Limit Representation? Paper presented at annual meeting of the Western Political Science Association, Portland, OR.

Wright, J. R. 1985. PACs, Contributions, and Roll Calls: An Organizational Perspective. *American Political Science Review* 79: 400-414.

———. 1990. Contributions, Lobbying, and Committee Voting in the U.S. House of Representatives. *American Political Science Review* 84: 417-38.

Zupan, M. A. 1990. The Last Period Problem of Politics: Do Congressional Representatives Not Subject to a Reelection Constraint Alter Their Voting Behavior? *Public Choice* 65: 167-80.

Index

groups, 82-84, 87-91, 92n5;
knowledge of constituents, 39-44,
83; legislative activity, 62-63;
motivations, 15; substantive
representation, 49-55, 56n6
public opinion, 1, 5, 9, 81-82

race. *See* Congress members'
characteristics and constituents
Reingold, B., 8
representation, 7-10, 54, 70, 93-94;
defined, 7; delegate, 9, 21n3, 51,
53, 91; elections, 15-16; ethics,
73-75; interest groups, 82; scope,
9, 23, 37-38; trustee, 9, 21n3, 54,
88; types, 7-9, 20, 21n2, 44, 48.
See also descriptive
representation; substantive
representation
retrospective citizen legislator, 2, 92-
98; activity, 62-63; ambition, 14-
15; constituent interests, 11-12,
48; contacting constituents, 39-44;
defined, 6, 18-19; descriptive
representation, 26-33;
effectiveness, 13, 58-70; elections,
16, 38; ethics, 12-13, 75-79;
ideology, 49-50; interest groups,
82-84, 87-91; party support, 49-
55; substantive representation, 49-
55
Riley, Rep. Bob, 20, 53, 77
Roukema, Rep. Marge, 14
Rohde, D. W., 35n7, 61
roll-call votes, 46, 48-55, 95. *See also*
voting participation
Roemer, Rep. Tim, 83
Romano, L., 77
Rosenstone, S. J., 28
Rosenthal, A., 12
Rosenthal, H., 55n3
rotation in office. *See* term limits
Rothenberg, L. S., 16, 46, 59

Sanders, M. S., 16, 46, 59
Sanford, Rep. Mark, 20, 43, 54, 73, 77,
88
Schlesinger, J. A., 6, 13, 38, 46
Scott, Rep. Robert, 86
seniority. *See* experience

Sensenbrenner, Rep. James, 1
Shadegg, Rep. John, 78
Shelby, Rep. Richard, 37
Shepsle, K. A., 60
Smith, E. R. N., 46
Smith, R. Jeffery, 86
Smith, S., 60
Snyder, Rep. Victor, 77
substantive representation, 46-55, 73,
95. *See also* representation
staff, 10, 38, 40-44, 97-98
state legislatures, 12, 15-16, 18-19, 39,
95
state legislative experience, 58
Stavernagel, G. A., 25
Stein, R. M., 15, 39
Stewart, C., III, 27, 75
Stokes, D. E., 24, 46
Swain, C. M., 8
Swears, M. L., 8

Tate, K., 8-10
Taylor A. J., 57
Tedin, K., 27
Terkildsen, H., 26
term limits: constituent contact, 16, 39,
95, 97; debate, 14, 16, 22n9;
effectiveness, 57; federalist, 2;
legislator's motives, 14-15, 46;
movement, 1, 5; pledge, 3, 17, 53,
73; removal, 2, 22n11; women,
11, 22n6. *See also* prospective
citizen legislator
Theiss-Morse, E., 82
Thomas, N., 28
Thomas, S., 8, 15, 25, 46, 60
Thompson, D. F., 10, 74-76, 82
Thurmond, Sen. Strom, 73
Tien, C., 8
Tolbert. C. J., 8
Traficant, Rep. Jim, 75
Trips, fact-finding. *See* junkets
trips to district, 10, 16, 38, 40-44, 97-98
Trump, Donald, 79
Tyler, T. R., 74

U.S. Term Limits, 17
U.S. Term Limits, Inc. v. Thornton, 5,
22n11

About the Authors

Rebekah Herrick is an associate professor in political science at Oklahoma State University. Her recent publications focus on congressional ethics, political ambition, and gender and politics.

Samuel H. Fisher III is an associate professor in political science at the University of South Alabama. Besides Congress, he has also written on southern politics and Québec politics.